PSYCHOLOGY OF ENGINEERING CREATIVITY

Psychology of Engineering Creativity

DR. MANJIT SEN GUPTA
National Council of Educational Research and Training,
New Delhi

A FALCON BOOK From COSMO PUBLICATIONS

NEW DELHI INDIA

1984

Psychology of Engineering Creativity

First Published 1984

Published by :
Rani Kapoor (Mrs.)
For **FALCON Books**
Parent Company
COSMO PUBLICATIONS
24-B Ansari Road,
New Delhi-110002, (India)

Printed at :
Parashar Printers,
New Seelampur, Delhi-110053

FOREWORD

The study which follows is much more than just another creativity study in yet another cultural context. It is, instead, devoted to educing evidence regarding a number of the very basic issues which underlie research in this complex but important area. Perhaps foremost among these issues is a question regarding the relationship between intelligence and creativity. A second and comparable concern has to do with identifying some of the major correlates of creativity, and with the fundamental dimensions which could account for the observed relationships among the measures of these correlates. Third, one must necessarily be interested in the relative importance of the various predictors of creativity, and with the statistical significance of their criterion correlations. Dr. Gupta addresses all of these issues, and a number of others, on the pages which follow. In addition, he does this in a fashion so thorough and scholarly as to argue that his book must be viewed as required reading for any serious student of creativity.

Georgia, U.S.A.

William A. Owens
Director
The University of Georgia
Institute for Behavioral Research,
Athens, Georgia 30602 U.S.A.

PREFACE

The purpose of the present study, conducted by Dr. Sen Gupta is to examine the inventive and innovative potential of engineering students. Education and training programmes for prospective technicians and engineers can be effectively restructured in favour of invention and innovation only if serious research findings are available about cognitive, motivational and personological characteristics of creative engineers particularly in the Indian context. This is precisely the attempt that this book makes in the pages that follow. Alongwith the main problem investigated in this volume it presents up-to-date research findings in the area of engineering creativity done in India and abroad.

To make the book more useful Dr. Sen Gupta has added a chapter entitled "The Training of Creative Thinking" which provides details about some promising techniques for developing creativity. He maintains that 'creativity can be learned by the person for whom it does not come "naturally".' Research on 'teachability' of creativity, in fact, is opening new possibilities for mankind.

In my opinion the book will be of great use to students and research scholars in the fields of psychology and education. Besides, it will be of particular interest to engineering educators as well. It will also be of much interest to persons in other fields concerned with understanding and developing creative imagination.

DR. M.K. RAINA
National Institute of Education,
NCERT New Delhi.

PREFACE

The purpose of the present study conducted by Dr. Sen Gupta is to examine the inventive and innovative potential of engineering students. Education and training programmes for prospective technicians and engineers can be effectively restructured in favour of invention and innovation only if serious research findings are available about cognitive, motivational and personological characteristics of creative engineers, particularly in the Indian context. This is precisely the attempt that the book makes in the pages that follow. Alongwith the main problem investigated in this volume it gives an up-to-date research findings in the area of engineering creativity done in India and abroad.

To make the book more useful Dr. Sen Gupta has added a chapter entitled "The Training of Creative Thinking" which provides details about some promising techniques for developing creativity. He maintains that creativity can be developed in a person for whom it does not come naturally. Research on teachability of creativity, in fact, is opening new possibilities for mankind.

In my opinion the book will be of great use to students and research scholars in the fields of psychology and education. Besides it will be of particular interest to engineering educators as well. It will also be of much interest to persons in other fields concerned with understanding and developing creative imagination.

Dr. M.K. RAINA
National Institute of Education
NCERT New Delhi

ACKNOWLEDGEMENT

The author would like to express his deep sense of gratitude to his research guides Dr. M.K. Raina of National Council of Educational Research and Training, New Delhi and Dr. A.P. Sharma of N.A.S. College, Meerut for their expert guidance and supervision.

The researcher is grateful to Prof. C.V. Govinda Rao, formerly Head, Vocationalization of Education Unit, NCERT, New Delhi who has been a source of inspiration and encouragement to him.

The author also greatly appreciates the publication grant provided by the National Council of Educational Research and Training (NCERT) which was a welcome assistance.

Appreciation is also expressed to the Purdue Research Foundation, USA for the permission granted to use the 'Purdue Creativity Test' in this thesis.

The author also wishes to acknowledge the help provided by Shri R. Sen Gupta of Indian Railways ; Shri V.K. Jain of NCERT ; Anindya K. Mukherjee of Engineers India Limited in processing the data and Dr. Uma Shanker of Management Development Institute for sending valuable material concerning 'The Budner Tolerance-Intolerance of Ambiguity Scale.'

Perhaps the greatest indebtedness is to the student-subjects and to the Principals, Heads of Mechanical and Electrical Engineering Departments of the polytechnics of Delhi and their lecturers who cordially extended their cooperation for conducting this study.

The author wants to place on record his debt to all those authors and researchers whose works have been consulted and quoted.

The researcher, of course, wishes to record his thankfulness to his wife, Mrs. Shaon Sengupta and his son Satyajit for providing active assistance and stimulating environment throughout the study.

The author wishes to express his gratitude to the ICSSR for providing the contingency grant to conduct this investigation.

New Delhi **MANJIT SEN GUPTA**

CONTENTS

LIST OF TABLES

LIST OF CHARTS

CHAPTER I

Nature of Engineering Creativity

Creativity : Its meaning and definition

Man is a free agent (*Swatantra Karta*), and creativity functions within his nature—within human nature rests the capacity to go beyond what is. Man, then, is the bearer of the creative process. "He is a unique representation of the universe in whom the unconscious creativity of nature becomes conscious creativity" (Radhakrishnan, 1960). Every person has been endowed with the spark of creativity, which he tries to express in one way or the other. There was an erroneous notion which the modern psychologists have disproved that creativity is the "sole prerogative" of few selected individuals. In the 1962 ASCD Year book the authors state : "Creativity is in each of us . . . This idea is comforting in that it gives us a measure of hope as we work with individuals; it is disturbing in that it points up how much we have yet to learn about this intangible and illusive phenomenon". Heist (1968) rightly warned : If deplorable waste of human talent is to be prevented and if creatively gifted students are not to choose the paths of delinquency, mental illness, or at best a life of mediocrity and unrealised potentialities it becomes essential that serious attempts are made to identify creative talent.

Creativeness, in the best sense of the word, requires two things : an original concept, or "idea", and a benefit to someone

(Mason, 1960). Although considerable improvements giving substantial benefit or other human satisfaction may be obtained by the routine engineering procedures, creative ability is shown by some contribution which is beyond the routine or obvious and which, in one or more aspects, must be relevant to and critical in obtaining the desired result, eigher in terms of quantity or quality. Hallman (1963) has analysed the creative act into five major components : (1) it is a whole *act*, a unitary instance of behaviour ; (2) it terminates in the production of *objects* or of forms of living which are distinctive ; (3) it evolves out of certain *mental processes ;* (4) it co-varies with specific *personality transformation ;* and (5) it occurs within a particular kind of environment.

Numerous reviews (Davis, Manske & Train, 1967 ; Golann 1963 ; Hahn, 1968 ; Mooney, 1957 ; Taylor, 1964) indicate that creativity has been studied traditionally as a cognitive *process* or as a *product* which reflects the underlying creative process. Four viewpoints are relevant to the *process* orientation : *definitional, dispositional, psychoanalytic* and *humanistic* approaches. The *definitional* approach is least rigorous of all, consisting essentially of introspective opinions and hunches regarding the nature of the creative process. The *dispositional* (personality) approach employs questionnaires, personality inventories (e.g. Gough's 1960, Adjective Checklist), interviews, "living-in" assessments and other dispositional indicators such as intelligence and cognitive style measures. The *psychoanalytic* approach, the third major process orientation, gains impetus from traditional psychoanalysis and neo-Freudian sources. Last, the *humanistic* approach (e.g. Maslow, Rogers) is less deterministic than traditional psychoanalysis, treating creativity as one manifestation of self-actualization or man's constant, dynamic fulfilment of his inherent potentialities.

The creative product orientation includes both the S—R *behaviouristic* and the *operational* approaches. The most common research technique of *behaviouristic* approach is verbal association employed as an independent training variable (Maltzman, 1960) or as a dependent measure (Mednick, 1962). The *operational* approach, more than any other, places emphasis upon training creativity.

It seems evident from the above that no fully matured, comprehensive theoretical statement has been developed which is directed specifically toward creativity. Existing explanatory constructs rely upon large, established systems such as S—R behaviourism and Freudian psychology. Undoubtedly, psychology is long overdue for a direct and detailed theory of creativity.

Creativity has been defined in a variety of ways, ranging from an attitude that can exist though nothing is created to the production of high level and relatively infrequent accomplishments in culturally significant areas of behaviour. Fromm (1959) defines the conditions of creativity as the capacity for wonder, the capacity to face incongruity and tension, to orient oneself towards the new, to be aware of experience and to respond fully to such awareness. Definitions like this make no reference to achievement or productivity : they focus on the abilities, attitudes, personal attributes and experiences thought to precede creative productivity. Creative products are visible proof of the potential and are usually the most practical, starting point for the investigator. Parnes (1966) defines creative behaviour as 'behaviour which demonstrates both uniqueness and value in its product.' Different definitions of creativity, in one form or another, involve the capacity to make products, either tangible or intangible, which are both new and valuable. "The product and the process are both important. Without the process there would be no product. With the product . . . . —there might not be more than fantasy. . . ." Brunelle (*Kaiser Aluminium News,* 1968). The path of creative insight is often thin and dim. It is not a happening in which some abstraction bursts full blown into consciousness ; it is the result of intensive effort at seeking new structures of known information of a long mixing of ideas often "felt" rather than cognized. It is only the jelling that we "know". (Merrifield, 1976).

Torrance (1965) described creativity as the process of becoming sensitive to problems, deficiencies, gaps in knowledge, missing elements, disharmonies, and so on ; identifying the difficulty ; searching for solutions, making guesses, or formulating hypotheses about the deficiencies ; testing and retesting these hypotheses and possibly modifying and retesting them ; and finally communicating the results.

This definition lists four ways in which people behave creatively. The first behaviour is the process of sensing difficulties, being aware of problems, or of missing elements in information. This is an evaluative thinking process. The second behaviour is that of formulating hypotheses, making guesses, asking questions, investigating and manipulating information. This is the divergent thinking process which consists of the abilities of being fluent, flexible, original and elaborative. The third is another evaluative process which calls for testing and revising those hypotheses, guesses, or questions which occurred as the second step of process. Here again, the mental abilities of setting criteria, judging, modifying, retesting and remaining flexible come into play. The last behaviour is that of communicating the results to others. This is based upon the study of creative individuals who possess the trait of wanting to tell others about their discovery, invention or innovation. Torrance prefers this definition because it is equally useful in all areas of the curriculum, in mathematics, the sciences, languages, the arts, social studies, music, physical education, psychology and human relations. Such a definition places creativity in the realm of daily living and does not reserve it for ethereal and rarely achieved heights of creations.

Traditional S--R theory would predict that the emission of original ideas should increase with practice and reinforcement. According to Staats (1968), creativity occurs when two or more stimuli, which normally do not elicit one another as mediating stimulus events, become associated. The "creative" association results from stimuli presented in spatial and temporal contiguity. Mednick (1962) presenting another associative interpretation of creativity confronted with the notion of *incubation* defined as "a stage of the process during which no active attempts at solution are being made but which nevertheless results in improvement of performance." Although behaviourism as applied to creativity has helped in the study of the latter, the reduction of creativity to learned associations presents a simplistic and incomplete picture of this complex human behaviour.

Creativity, in one of the earliest theoretical descriptions, was said to result from the sublimation of libidinal energy from sexual activities to asexual goals. Through sublimation, energy is invested in socially approved scientific, artistic, and ideological activities ; creativity thus represents a ready escape into "fantasy life" void of frustration and anxeity. Many later theorists, however, renounced the traditional Freudianism either because of inconsistencies or because the traditional theory handled certain data inadequately. The analysis of complex creative processes demanded more specific elaboration.

Humanistic psychologists consider creativity a naturally evolving component of "psychological health". According to them creativity is not the pessimistic avoidance of anxiety through fantasy, but rather the process of direct and deliberate confrontation between self and environment. The humanistic construct, unlike the psychoanalytic, sees creativity as depending not upon causes occurring solely in childhood, but also on those actualized in present experiences. Rogers (1962) found that creativity is encouraged by a milieu of *psychological safety* and *psychological freedom*. The creative individual displays openness to experience, an internal locus of evaluation, and an ability to "toy" with elements.

Personality factors, instead of achievements and products, are the key to Maslow's (1958) version of "self actualizing" creativity. Characteristics of self-actualizing personality are boldness, courage, freedom, spontaneity, perspicuity, integration and self-acceptance. Creative individuals are psychologically healthy, capable of voluntary "regression" but not "compulsive-obsessive" nor fearful of novelty. Humanistic psychologists, thus, exhibit certain important biases not present in other analyses, particularly the emphasis upon the fulfilment of man's potentialities as the most important basic need of human development.

The dispositional approach, like the psychoanalytic, examines creativity as a facet of personality or intellectual development. It employs procedures, techniques, and controls similar to those used in experimental psychology. Barron (1962, 1969) conceptualized creativity as a complex measurable, normally-distributed personality trait. His studies through personality inventories, projective tests, aesthetic preference measures and others profiled creative individuals as mentally "healthy", more observant of others, valuing truthful and explicit reporting, more energetic in behaviour, more flexible in the perception of themselves and others, apparently more given to complexity, fantasy, and imaginative thoughts, highly sensitive to synthesis and exacting discrimination, aware of their own and others' feelings, questioning the implicit, preferring the complex and asymmetrical in general, more "psycho-dynamically complex."

Structure of intellect

The beginning of the modern interest in creativity by general psychologists is usually dated to a 1950 presidential address to the American Psychological Association by J.P. Guilford in which he eloquently emphasised the need for research in this area. Guilford (1950, 1962) introduced experimental psychology to the scientific study of creativity through his classic *structure of intellect model.*

IQ tests commonly emphasise abilities in the operation categories of cognition, memory, and convergent production, ignoring divergent production and slighting evaluation abilities, the latter being the basic aspects of critical thinking. Creativity, or divergent thinking, involves the production of many solutions, and is contrasted with convergent thinking, the tendency to "converge" upon a single problem solution. Guilford has factor analytically identified (a) sensitivity to problems, (b) word fluency, (c) ideational fluency, (d) associational fluency, (e) expressional fluency, (f) spontaneous flexibility, (g) adaptive *flexibility*, and (h) originality as important components of divergent thinking. Getzles and Jackson drew heavily upon the Guilford measures for their study of creativity and intelligence.

In point of fact, as indicated, no single approach sufficiently explains all or even most of the important facets of creativity. Creative behaviour is complex, affected by multitudes of presently undefined developmental and environmental influences and encompassing numerous and varied modes of expression, In sum, the present state of the art is a mixture of some models, limited applications, operational and non-operational definitions, random speculation, and some hypothesis testing. Progress, to date, is promising, but manifestly incomplete. Nonetheless, creativity is coming of age.

Creativity and innovation in engineering

Relating creativity to engineering Blade (1963) observes :

> In a sense every engineering achievement may be considered creative if we rule out repeat problems with repeat solutions. This is true to the extent that we consider any outcome creative if it is new and original (although some investigators such as Bronowski, in considering the highest type of creative endeavours "perception in disorder of a deep new unity", would not consider the inventions, clever rearrangement, and problem solving of the engineer as highly creative). However, this is the nature of most of the creativity of the engineer. He designs and constructs something new and original, and creativity in engineering is the mental process of conceptualizing and envolving such a design.

Engineers are essential instruments of technological innovation ; technological innovation, all knowledgeable parties seem to agree, becomes an increasingly vital factor in the achievement of domestic and international goals (National Conference on Creative Engineering Education, 1965). This Conference, therefore, recommended that the development of the inventive and innovative potential of engineering students should be an active concern of industry, government, the universities, and in larger perspective, society as a whole. Professor M.W. Thring (1968) of Leeds has introduced the concept of "complete engineers". Education of such engineers should be organised in a way that their natural inventiveness is developed to the point where they cannot only think up quite new processes and products of real value to humanity, but also overcome all the obstacles in the way of producing a successful realization of these products. Engineering education should encourage students to strive for the mastery of fundamentals, the discovery of the relatedness of things, and the cultivation of excellence. But all the while it should also be a creative experience, stimulating the imagination of students and helping them to prepare themselves for the unresolved contests and the new challenges of an imperfect world. In a similar context, Professor Swani (1975), erstwhile Director, Indian Institute of Technology, New Delhi, in his welcome address to the Golden Jubilee Session of the Association of Indian Universities stressed that good engineering and technical education should develop the creative abilities in engineering students for tackling unforeseen problems and for the speedy development of our industrial potential—Nagarajan (1973). The Finniston Report on the Engineering Profession in the U.K. (1980) also drew attention to the need to develop programmes for the 'formation' of engineers with an emphasis on the development of practical abilities, synthesis and creativity, and commitment to the notion of engineering practice in a commercial e.g. manufacturing environment. In Czechoslovakia too at the 10th FEANI Seminar on the "Promotion of creative activities of engineers" Goodyear (1979) stressed :

> The problem of stimulating the creativity of engineers and scientists is a key one for all countries, for the developing countries and for the industrialised countries. For economic and social development to occur, it is essential that our engineers be able to innovate, to explore new paths towards better solutions of engineering problems, to make use of new scientific advances, and to exploit new tools that are becoming available.

But unfortunately, engineering educators as a group have not yet been concerned with the problems of creativity. There are deeply held feelings that engineering eduction today has become too science-based and has become removed to some degree from the creative act that the engineer or inventor has to perform to bring the results of science and technology to the benefit of society. Although engineering by its nature is a creative endeavour the identification of creative talent and its stimulation in the classroom are not yet recognised as the tasks of engineering educators.

Engineering is epitomised in the process of invention and innovation (De Simone, 1968). Engineering by its very nature is creative. In many definitions of creativity and engineering one can notice a generic relationship. Offner (1967), Professor of Mechanical Engineering at Illinois, has defined creativity as a dynamic process for obtaining a realizable solution to a need. This process occurs in a mental reactor, is fired by imagination, controlled by reason, and results in critical fusing for the first time of selected elements from a stockpile of knowledge and experience. The first of the six themes commonly shared at Woodshole (De Simone, 1968) has been that invention and innovation are the essence of creative engineering. Without the problem-solving characteristics and the ability to synthesise and evolve new and improved engineering configurations in the service of man (Gregory, 1971), an engineer is nothing more than a living store-house of factual knowledge (Krick, 1965). But paradoxically this art of creative engineering has been orphaned in the engineering and technical schools. In fact, in creative engineering education, education for innovation should be the first and foremost objective.

If engineering educators are interested in the development of new products and original ideas, the educational techniques they utilize must seek to apply what is currently known about the creative person and process. To date, however, there is little knowledge as to how to develop the potential creativity and creative traits of students in an engineering programme (Williams, 1966). This is because the public and educators do not have well defined and authentic information regarding the characteristics of creative engineers. In this context Blade (1963) has also observed that "There is little notion of creative engineer in the minds of the public, although the image of the creative scientist is widespread . . . . (E)ngineers are anonymous." In the literature too, relatively little had been devoted to the creative scientist or engineer as such (Whitfield, 1975). What exists "provides considerable overlap and plenty of contradiction".

Identifying personal characteristics of engineers

From among the variety of studies on creativity there is an emerging notion that creative products arise from a combination of factors which include individuals with preferred intellectual characteristics and more particularly, with preferred personality characteristics, aspects of the immediate work-environment and the regional and social background. In other words, no single parameter is adequate in explaining creative work in any field. Engineering is no exception to this view. According to McPherson (1967) creative engineers are dedicated to solving problems, pursuing their goals aggressively though quietly, are non-conformist in their ideas, and are childlike and uninhibited in seeking ideas to test. At other times they exhibit extremely rigorous and scientific behaviour, tackle obstacles vigorously and show a general dissatisfaction with themselves and the world around them.

Donald Mackinnon (1969) in his paper, "The Courage to Be : Realising Creative Potential", states : If one would attempt to give the briefest summary of a creative person, one might say that he appears to be distinguished, most generally, by two fundamental traits, one intellective, and the other motivational or attitudinal. Creativity, in other words, is not entirely a cognitive process, nor is it entirely the result of a complex set of personality traits. Creativity, perhaps, can become a style of life when there will be interpretation and interweaving of these so-called subjective and so-called objective factors (Hacker, 1965). The assessment of creative potential should, therefore, include not only singular intellectual characteristics but also cognitive styles and personality variables. Creativity, it has been amply demonstrated, cannot happen in a vacuum. It, to some extent, is an unusual recombination and reorganization of experiences and is a matter of utilising a variety of associations accessible to an individual.

Above average intelligence

One of the cognitive capacities that appear to be most frequently associated with the creative is an above-average intelligence and the effective use of this intelligence. It is the capacity for abstract thinking (Terman, 1921). Operationally speaking, it is the aggregate or global capacity of the individual to act purposefully, to think rationally, and to deal effectively with his environment (Wechsler, 1958). Mackinnon (1967) describes intelligent person as more discerning (more observant in a differentiated fashion), more alert (can concentrate attention readily and shift it appropriately), and more fluent in scanning thoughts and producing those which meet some problem-solving criterion. Such a person will generally have more information (in the most general sense of the term) at his command. Furthermore, items of information he possesses may more readily enter into combinations among themselves, and the number of possible combinations is increased for such a person because of the greater information and the greater fluency of combination. Since true creativity is defined by the adaptiveness or a response as well as its unusualness, it is apparent that intelligence alone will tend to produce greater creativity.

Gowan (1969) considered intelligence as a necessary condition for creative performance since it provides the vocabulary to be sorted and the means of selection One reason why children of lower intelligence rarely became creative is that they do not reach Bruner's symbolic representation. In contrast the bright child reaches this stage about the middle of this period when the creative motivations cog-itate or "shake together" the symbolic representations of experience.

Concerning intelligence and creativity Anastasi and Schaefer

(1971) proposed "that the term 'creativity', like the the term 'intelligence', be recognised as referring to a loosely defined, broad, and many-faceted concept. Both terms will undoubtedly survive as independent concepts because they provide convenient short-cuts in designating complex behaviour domains of considerable practical importance. But neither corresponds to a precisely defined or distinct entity. Each comprises a multiplicity of identifiable traits, organised in a pattern of relationships that cuts across the two domains".

Many researchers (Getzels & Jackson, 1962 ; Torrance, 1962, 1964 ; Anastasi and Schaefer, 1971 ; Hasan & Butcher, 1966 ; Wallach & Kogan, 1965 and others) have investigated whether there is a correlation between intelligence and creativity. There is as yet no unanimous consent on the matter. The extent to which 'intelligent' and 'creative' describe independent traits is still hotly debated. Some studies suggest very little overlap, others indicate that the two are virtually indistinguishable. Given the controversy over the relationship between creativity and intelligence, it is interesting to note that Belbin (1981) generally found his most creative contributors to be in the top 20% of his managerial population on critical thinking ability, as assessed by performance on the Watson-Glaser Critical Thinking Appraisal.

However, to date there is little doubt that tests of general intelligence, although imperfect, have proved more useful in practice than any other kind of psychological test.

"All available research support the conclusion that the correlation between measures of creativity and intelligence is positive but low (.20—.40) in general unselected population and practically zero in the selected populations" (Yamamoto, 1961). Therefore, the prevailing opinion is that although creative people are intelligent persons, an exceptionally high IQ is not a pre-requisite for creativity. On the contrary, it may inhibit the inner resources of the individual. However, results are contradictory and no definite evidence is available about the role of intelligence in creativity in engineering.

Specific reasoning ability

Creativity, in technical and engineering fields, perhaps, also requires certain amount of knowledge and competence in the relevant work, an involvement in its process and a sensitivity to the requirements of the particular branch of engineering. Maddi (1965) made a point when he argued that both quality and novelty are essential for creative production. The motivational and personological qualities are not individually sufficient for creative production. A preference for complexity, for example, without the added qualities of competence in the relevant work is hardly likely to lead to products which are at once original and adequate In one of his letters to M.K. Raina, William A. Owens wrote that "mechanical comprehension should be an integral part of engineering creativity." Mechanical reasoning, therefore, is perhaps an important underlying cognitive ability for doing creative problem-solving in mechanical engineering. But this hypothesis has not been tested as yet.

Value system

Numerous theories have been advanced to explain motivational factors which stimulate individuals towards creative productivity. Psychologists have conceived the basic interests or motives in personality under the term 'value' and their attempts to classify individuals on the basis of values have met with success in a number of studies (Allport *et al,* 1960). Values have been described as "ideas-tied-to-feelings". They denote the attitude of prizing a thing, finding it worthwhile for its own sake, or intrinsically on the one hand and a distinctively intellectual act—an operation of comparing, judging or evaluating on the other. In other words, values represent an individual's philosophy that guides him in his behaviour under a variety of situations.

Values are essentially related to social interaction and represent the systematised reaction tendencies on the part of the individual. Emphasising the importance of study of values

Stein (1953) suggested that a society encourages creativity to the extent its value system includes a positive regard for change and novelty. It discourages creativity to the extent that social pressures for conformity are so intense that deviations are punished directly or indirectly through social ostracism.

Problems, however, arise from conflicting values. For example the economic attitude comes into conflict with other values. Its utility principle conflicts with the aesthetic values, except when art serves commercial ends. The aesthetic attitude on its part is in a sense diametrically opposed to the theoretical ; the former is concerned with the diversity and the latter with the identities of experience. McKinnon and his associates at the IPAR found creative architects entertaining both theoretical and aesthetic values, although, as discussed above, for many people, perhaps most, there is some incompatibility and conflict between a cognitive and rational concern with truth and an emotional concern with form and beauty. When there is conflict, it would appear that the creative individual has the capacity to tolerate the tension created in him by strong opposing values, and in his life and work, he effects some reconciliation of them.

Though a study of values has been made mostly by IPAR group with various groups of eminent people but sufficient information is not available about value-orientation of creative engineers. These relatively unexplored research problems in addition to others were the basis for the present investigation.

Perceptual preference for complexity

Creativity is also a function of style or modes of experiencing, or stylistic ways of using the mind (Barron, 1971). There are three distinct stylistic variables that have been found consistently to mark the highly creative person. Two of these are drawn from Jung's theory of psychological types, and the third rests upon the polar opposition between perference for phenomenal complexity and asymmetry and perference for simplicity and symmetry.

It may be described briefly as à bi-polar factor which opposes a preference for perceiving and dealing with complexity to a preference for perceiving and dealing with simplicity, when both of these alternatives are phenomenally present and when a choice must be made between them.

Preference for simplicity is associated with social conformity, respect for custom and ceremony, friendliness toward tradition, somewhat categorical moral judgment, an undeviating patriotism, and suppression of such troublesome new forces as inventions that would temporarily cause unemployment. Complexity goes along with artistic interests, unconventionality, political radicalism, high valuation of creativity and a liking for change.

The types of preceptual preference as observed by Barron (1963) are related basically to a choice of what to attend to in the complex of phenomena that makes up the world of experience; for the world is both stable and unstable, predictable and unpredictable, ordered and chaotic. To see it predominantly as one or the other is a sort of perceptual decision One may attend to its ordered aspect, to regular sequences of events, to a stable centre of the universe or one may instead attend primarily to the eccentric, the relative, and the arbitrary aspect of the world.

At its best, the decision in favour of order makes for personal stability and balance, a sort of easy-going optimism combined with religious faith, a friendliness toward tradition, custom and ceremony and respect for authority without subservience to it. At its worst, the decision in favour of order makes for categorical rejection of all that threatens disorder, a fear of anything that might bring disequilibrium Optimism becomes a matter of policy, religion a prescription and a ritual. Such a decision is associated with stereotyped thinking rigid and compulsive morality, and hatred of instinctual aggressive and erotic forces which might upset the precariously maintained balance.

The decision in favour of complexity, at its best, makes for originality and creativeness, a greater tolerance for unusual ideas and formulations. The sometimes disordered and unstable world has its counterpart in the person's inner discord, but the crucial ameliorative factor is a constant effort to integrate the inner and outer complexity in a higher order synthesis. The goal is to achieve the psychological analogue of mathematical elegance: to allow into the perceptual system the greatest possible richness of experience, while yet finding in this complexity some overall pattern. Such a person is not immobilized by anxiety in the face of great uncertainty, but is at once perturbed and challenged. For such an individual, optimism is impossible, but pessimism is lifted from the personal to the tragic level, resulting not in apathy but in participation in the business of life. At its worst, such a perceptual attitude leads to grossly disorganized behaviour, to a surrender to chaos. It results in nihilism, despair, and disintegration.

Barron (1971) on the basis of extensive studies in the field of preceptual preferences observed that one of their most important findings and probably the one most solidly supported by diverse kinds of evidence has to do with the relationship of complexity to simplicity, and of order to disorder. It has been observed consistently that individuals identified as more highly creative have the capacity to integrate the richness of experience into a higher order synthesis that makes for the unusual in creative production or performance. They prefer complexity *i.e.* they have a strong desire to turn disorder into meaning, to accept innovation and the challenge presented by apparent imperfection. This dimension of personality, namely, the perceptual simplicity-complexity has not been sufficiently explored in relation to creativity and particularly as related to creativity in engineers, though Snyder (1967) has made comparison using complexity scale between science and engineering students studying at M.I.T.

Openness to new ideas

Benson Snyder (1967) in his large scale study introduced 'tolerance' and 'intolerance' for ambiguity as a distinctive concept in the development of creative thinking. The acceptance and tolerance of ambiguity, as defined by Budner (1962) is the tendency of the individual to perceive ambiguous, more complex and unstructured situations as desirable and gratifying. Such an individual is open-minded who tries to perceive a situation, however vague it may be, in terms of the objective characteristics of the situation itself rather than in terms of certain pre-conceived notions and subjectively recognized categories. He prefers, therefore, to postpone his judgment, or tolerate ambiguity of the situation till such time as is required to understand the situation in terms of objective characteristics inherent in the situation itself rather than in terms of ready-made concepts and subjectively recognized categories, which may be irrelevant to the understanding of the situation as it objectively stands. In contrast, a closed minded individual on account of his tendency to disregard such objective characteristics of situation as are inconsistent with, or contrary to his pre-conceived notions and subjectively recognized categories regarding the situation, instead of postponing his judgment and tolerating the ambiguity of the situation, readily and hastily defines and constructs the situation not in terms of the inherent characteristics of the situation itself but in terms of his own subjective notions and categories.

The term intoleranee of ambiguity was first used by Else-Frenkel Brunswik (1949) to explain the phenomenon of ambivalence, that is, the conflict of favourable and unfavourable feelings which, according to psychoanalysis, a child in Oedipus Complex situation tends to show towards his parents. The child has to become more comfortable with ambiguity. He must learn to separate it from anxiety. In life there is often more than one answer to a question, and if a question is not well put, there may be no answer at all. The child has to live with this kind of intellectual tension without becoming affectively anxious about it and without aborting the creative ideas which produce it.

Openness to ideas is a characteristic of the creative person. He is able to tolerate conceptual ambiguity : is not made anxious by configural disorder, but sees in it a clue to a higher synthesis. Barron (1958) found in his investigations that the creatives tolerated disorder better and were more able to find unity in disorder in drawings than others. They were more open to innovation and less disturbed by surface imbalance.

The highly creative is able to tolerate apparent confusion or ambiguity for a longer period than the poor creative. He is capable of existing amidst a state of affairs in which he does not comprehend all that is going on, but he continues to effect resolution despite the present lack of homeostasis (Mooney and Razik, 1967).

Williams (1964) has also stressed that tolerance of ambiguity is one of the important motivational characteristics of the design engineer who is regarded as creative. He is further reported that one of the most consistent findings in many creativity studies among scientists and engineers is that the creative personality is perceptually "open". This implies a resistance to premature judgment. Faced with something new or different, the engineer searches for flaws, for signs of weakness, or for area of possible failure. The study of this dimension with mechanical engineers would further explain the role of tolerance of ambiguity in engineering.

CHAPTER II

Measurement of Engineering Creativity

When creativity is equated with genius and the process of creation is thought to be wholly mysterious, there is no need to develop the measurement of creativity. But when creativity is taken to be valued potentiality of all men and its development a valued social aim, then measurement becomes important (Money and Razik, 1967). In the context of research, there are two areas in which measurement is important : one is the area of "creative potential" and the other is the area of "creative performance" or creative production.

The dimensions of human personality which are likely to contribute to potential for the creativity can be conveniently categorized as motivational, temperamental, and attitudinal, which is to say that they are in the form of interests and attitudes, emotional dispositions, and abilities. Interests and attitudes should have most to do with whether or not the individual will direct his efforts toward innovative-productive behaviour, and if his efforts are so directed, what his choice of area of output will be (Guilford, 1967). Temperamental qualities should determine to some extent whether creative productivity and the directions of that productivity are congenial to the individuals' emotional disposition.

Different Approaches to Measurement of Engineering Creativity

Different approaches have been utilized in the effort to determine which traits seem to be relevant for creative potentialities. At the Institute for Personality Assessment and Research the major approach has been the study of groups of recognized creative producers, their comparisons with people not in such groups to note any significant differences in terms of test scores and other variables. Other investigators have taken the usual route of concurrent-validation studies, correlating trait evaluations with criteria designed to reflect creative performance in groups of scientists, public-relations individuals, advertising copy-writers, artists and the like. Very little has been done thus far toward conducting predictive validation studies.

Apart from the studies done with "men on the job" there have been some others with students as subjects. In these instances, the criteria have been in the form of ratings by observers of student behaviour or of products produced by the students. Guilford (1967) confirmed that the most meaningful and potentially useful dimensions of personality to use in measurement are those demonstrated to be unique by factor analysis. On the basis of his research culminating in the three dimensional model entitled 'the Structure of Intellect' Guilford (1950) stated the following hypotheses and assumptions basic to his model :

> Creativity represents patterns of primary abilities, patterns which can vary with different spheres of creative ability. Each primary ability is variable, along which individuals differ in continuous manner. Consequently, the nature of these abilities can be studied in people who are not necessarily distinguished for creative reasons. Productivity depends upon primary traits, including interests, aptitudes and temperamental variables. It is suggested that certain kinds of factors will be found including sensitivity to pro-

blems, ideational fluency, analyzing ability, recognition or redefining ability, span of ideational structure and evaluation ability.

Briefly, the abilities believed to be most relevant for creative thinking were identified by Guilford and associates as (a) Sensitivity to problems ; (b) Fluency of ideas ; (c) Originality (d) Redefinition (re-organisation, improvisation). These factors of creative thinking were part of the total gestalt of "known factors" which Guilford entitled the 'Structure of Intellect.' Although the divergent-production abilities seem logically most promising for assessing creative potentiality where aptitude is concerned, there are numerous other intellectual abilities in other operation categories—cognition, memory, convergent production and evaluation (Guilford, 1959 a ; Guilford, 1966 b) which are important.

Engineering is primarily concerned with producing results of value to people so that emphasis in measurement in engineering creativity must be placed upon the attainment of such results and their value. Therefore, it is to the solutions of engineering problems that one must look to decide whether creativity is manifest in a given situation. The problem solver—the engineer in this case—is influenced by behavioural, environmental and biographical factors to an unknown degree.

All successful engineering problem-solving produces a product. From the product it is possible to get measurable dimensions of creativity.

McPherson (1963) sets out a list of items which he saw as the basis of ultimate criteria for measuring creative output primarily in industrial scientific work :

TABLE 1

Proposals for Ultimate Criteria of Creative Scientific Output

1. Patents
2. Patent disclosures
3. Publications
4. Unpublished research reports

5. Unprinted oral presentations
6. Recorded ideas (any form)
7. Improved processes
8. New products
9. New Compounds
10. New Instruments
11. New analytical methods

Gregory (1972) however, pointed to a notable omission of any direct financial term in the above list. It is not impossible to get some measure of engineering creativity in money returns although such an assessment is likely to require a passage of considerable amount of time for the returns to come or else has to be based on assessments of likely return.

A creative engineer may be identified by direct products whose worth may be identified by secondary indicators of the type suggested by McPherson. Or he may be appraised in terms of his work style which supervisors might believe to be conducive to creative performance. Finally, he might be assessed in terms of his intellectual and personality variables which are believed to provide a basis for the production of creative contributions.

Tests for Measuring Engineering Creativity

Owens (1969), recently studied the effect of different factors on the prediction of creativity in machine design. For his subjects he concluded that the best leadership was by the example of their group head and their colleagues. It is notable in his results that the most influential single predictor was one aspect of the environment (technical style of the supervision), followed by a specific technological creativity test (number of solutions to a power source apparatus test), and then by a non-cognitive or motivational measure (favourable self-perception). His predictors were checked against practice. Getzels and Jackson (1962) and Wallach and Kogan (1965) developed tests of creativity in the 1960s but these Hudson (1966) regards as essentially measures of divergent thinking ability. Cattell

(1970), on the other hand approached the problem more empirically using his sixteen Personality Factor Questionnaire (16 PF). By comparing responses to the 16 PF from managers in selection and non-selection situations Elliott (1976) concludes that the "technically excellent instrument can be subject to distortion." Hartston (undated) developed "structured free response personality test". This, the Personal Preference Questionnaire (PPQ), is in effect a 'paired comparison' choice test, designated to be used in conjunction with other, more standard forms of personality inventory such as the 16 PF. Each response in the PPQ is classified under one of the twenty headings (or construct categories), and the spread of responses throughout the different categories is taken into account.

Richard H. Harris and A.L. Simberg (1959) of the AC Spark Plug Division of the General Motor Corporation developed the AC Test of Creative Ability. This test is a group paper and pencil test designed to give a measure or the quantity and the uniqueness of the ideas an individual can produce in a given situation. "As such, it can be used as an instrument for the selection of creative potential and, through the use of its two parallel forms, as an instrument to assess the degree to which creative thinking has been developed as a result of a training programme for this purpose." The developers of this test claim that the test has been widely used in the industry and used with over five thousand engineers and technical and supervisory personnel in the many divisions of the Grand Motors Corporation, and in industrial organisations concerned with manufacture of chemicals, pharmaceuticals, and office machinery and equipment. AC Test's two parallel forms consist of five parts as described in the Manual as follows :

Part I : A twenty-minute test containing five possible situations. The subject lists as many possible consequences of each situation as he can. This part yields both quantity and a uniqueness score.

Part II : A ten-minute test of general reasoning ability containing five usual and necessarily true statements. The subject lists as many reasons as possible to explain the truth of the statement. This part yields a quantity and uniqueness score.

Part III : A fifteen-minute test of sensitivity to problems, containing a list of five common appliances. The subject lists any improvements that he feels could be made in each one. This part yields a uniqueness score.

Part IV : A twenty-minute test of practical judgments containing five problem situations. The subject gives the solutions which he considers to be the least expensive and the least time-consuming. This part yields a single quantity score.

Part V : A fifteen-minute test of originality containing a list of five common objects. The subject gives as many possible uses as he can think of for each object. This part yields a quantity and a uniqueness score.

Buhl (1961) and others have used the AC Test of Creative Ability to study creative thinking among engineering students. Whittemore and Heimann (1966) also used it in their research. Lawshe and Harris (1960) developed the Purdue Creativity Test for measuring creativity in engineering. This test, has been included in *the Sixth Mental Measurements Year Book* by Buros (1965). "It was developed to aid in the selection and placement of engineering personnel in positions requiring the production of a number of original ideas for the solution of problems". The catalogue has recommended the test for identifying design engineers who "have the capacity to be really creative in the designs they produce" and research and development engineers "whose success depends upon the production of new ideas."

Perhaps there is no doubt that tests of creativity fail to measure certain processes which are continually in action, but sometimes, fundamentally unobservable (Barron), but still they can be useful atleast in identifying talents which may otherwise go waste. There is, however, a need to build a philosophically and empirically consistent theory about the measurement of creativity, which doesn't exist (Smith, 1968) and attempts to develop more adequate and well designed measures should continue indefinitely, which will prove of immense advantage to the educational engineer and researchers. In this context Guilford maintained : "if advancement of any science is proportional to the extent to which it has successfully applied measurement, then creativity as a science has not progressed considerably inspite of the hyperactivity in this field. But still some noteworthy attempts have been made to measure the creative mental functioning and "the quantification of creative behaviour has been a major step in a positive direction" (Khatena, 1971).

CHAPTER III

The Present Study

Creative Engineering has been defined as an insurance against capital loss. The needs of the future are tremendous and vision to plan that future is a commodity of even greater significance to the engineer today than it has ever been in the past (Rosen, 1958). Engineering today is being challenged to prepare the students to solve the future unknown problems. This challenge can be met only by selecting the potentially creative students as freshman engineers, restructuring the instructional programme of engineering education for developing creative talent among those preparing for engineering profession and developing teaching strategies for divergent thinking. All these changes can be introduced confidently only after having conducted considerable researches in the field of creativity in engineering, especially in Indian settings.

One might conceivably design engineering education programme not only to teach subject-matter content, but also to develop the creative traits or characteristics of the engineer. Such an education should provide abundant opportunities for the development of as many of these traits as possible while mastering subject-matter content at the same time. But there is not sufficient research available about cognitive, motivational and personological characteristics of creative engineers, which could help in designing the educational and training programme for prospective technicians and engineers. No such study has perhaps been attempted in this country (Mitra, 1972 ; Buch, 1974). It is this that has provided the necessary motivation for conducting this study.

There is often a profound belief that engineering is a version of science. It is because of this notion that much of the recent research in the field of technical creativity has been aimed at scientists rather than on engineers. Though it is difficult to distinguish between them in some of their day to day work, there are differences in their individual creative processes and in their creative products. Scientists are concerned with discovering and explaining nature; engineers use and exploit nature. Scientists are searching for theories and principles; engineers seek to develop and make things. Scientists are seeking result for its own ends; engineers are engaged in solving a problem for practical operating results. In his dramatic comparison Theodore Von Karmon said that while "the scientists explore what is. . . . the engineer creates what has never been". This is a different order of creativity (Blade, 1963).

From what is known in general about the relationship between thinking and behaviour, it can be expected with much certainty that an individual's personality plays an important role in his capacity to think and act creatively. To predict creativity to a high degree, one must get at a large number of different characteristics both intellectual and non-intellectual collectively to account for very much of the total creative performance. As a measurement area, the psychology of creativity cuts across the domains of perception, ideation, temperament and motivation (Barron, 1969).

A review of the studies conducted in the field of creative engineering reveals that there is a serious dearth of research studies, on qualities, characteristics and personality factors of creative engineers (Sen Gupta, 1976). Therefore, the state of knowledge in this area is poor. There is much to be explored in this area of engineering creativity so that the findings thus obtained could be applied in selecting proper type of students, developing enriched curricula, modifying teaching techniques in engineering institutions for turning out creative inquisitive and innovative engineering diplomats and graduates.

Henninger and Houghton (1970) in their comments concerning technical education in India at the polytechnic level submitted to the Ministry of Education, Govt. of India stated:

> It seems very clear that the prevailing interpretation of the officially prescribed syllabuses results in class-room and laboratory instruction of a rote-type which encourages the student to memorize what the teachers tell him and to copy facts, figures and diagrams neatly into note books, mostly without ever really studying or actually understanding much of any of the subject-matter.

Describing the present position of instructional processes in our polytechnics, Report on 'Institution Building Processes' from Technical Teachers Training Institute, Bhopal stressed that "Laboratory experiences there are stereotyped. Examples of innovative and developmental activitities are rare. . . ." This is because engineering educators in general educate largely by varying degrees of overemphasis on drill and grill, which interfere with the imaginative and creative processes. In fact, creativity rarely survives this educational grind.

In the context of a developing country like ours which is struggling hard to place itself on the forefront of technological advancement in a bid to successfully solve its problems of food, clothing, shelter, health, transportation, communication and energy, invention and innovation in the fields of engineering and technology becomes an increasingly vital factor (Sen Gupta, 1977). In this respect engineering schools and educators have to share greater responsibility to see that creativity is enthused and nurtured in the classrooms. This can only happen when ample research evidences are made available in such areas as identification of potential creativity, methods of teaching, personality and motivational characteristics, teaching-learning process etc. Country can march ahead only when its plans are backed by original, creative and talented band of engineers with enlightened vision, wide spectrum of creative ideas and ready to spearhead the future unknown challenges. It is in this context that Blade (1963) asked for continued research in identifying talented and creative engineers from the very beginning.

Objectives of the Study

The major objective of the present study is to compare quantitatively significant differences between high and low creative groups on certain measures of mechanical reasoning, perceptual simplicity-complexity, intolerance of ambiguity and value orientations.

Intrinsic to the central purpose of this study are the following sub-problems:

1. To investigate systematically differences in mechanical reasoning, which pertains to mechanical and physical principles in familiar situations, between high and low creative groups.
2. To compare differences between high and low creative groups on a measure of value orientations based on Spranger's theory of values.
3. To find out differences between high and low creative groups in their perception of cognitive simplicity and complexity.
4. To compare differences between high and low creative groups on a measure of intolerance of ambiguity.
5. To find out the contribution of each variable to the multiple correlation or more specifically the percentage of variance in the dependent variable (Total Creativity) accounted for by each of the ten predictor variables.
6. To rearrange or reduce the data by factor-analytic techniques to smaller set of factors or components that may be taken as source variables accounting for the observed interrelations in the data.
7. To determine the validity and reliability of the measure of creativity used in this study.
8. To determine the reliability of the measure of perceptual simplicity-complexity for the present study.

The Sample and the Setting

The sample selected for the study comprised of 522 students (all male) undergoing education and training in the area of Mechanical Engineering. These students were drawn from all the diploma-level engineering institutions in the Union Territory of Delhi. In the final analysis, however, a total of 400 students were studied who had responded to all the six instruments.

Definition of the Terms

The major terms used in this study are defined below in order to avoid ambiguity and the possibility of confusion:

Creativity

Creativity or creative thinking ability, in this study, will mean those operationally defined abilities measured by the paper and pencil test used (Purdue Creativity Test), and expressed accordingly by the subject's scores.

Fluency

This score is an indication of a subject's ability to think up as many possibilities as he can for each of the eight items (items 13-20) on the test depicted by line drawings.

Flexibility

This score is an indication of a subject's ability to think as many different possible uses or categories of uses as he can for each object (items 1-8) and two objects taken together (items 9-12) which are presented to him in the form of three dimensional drawings.

Intelligence

Intelligence in the present study will mean those operationally defined abilities which are measured by Cattell's Culture Fair Intelligence Test and are expressed accordingly by the subject's scores.

Mechanical Reasoning

It is an ability related to the learning of the principles of operation and repair of complex devices. The ability measured by the *Mechanical Reasoning Test* may be regarded as one aspect of intelligence, if intelligence is broadly defined.

Simplicity-Complexity

Perceptual simplicity-complexity is an important variable related to creative behaviour (Dallas and Gaier, 1970). It is the preference shown for simple or complex geometrical figures as measured by Chawla (1970) test of *Perceptual Simplicity-Complexity*.

Intolerance of Ambiguity

It is capacity to accept conflict and tension resulting from polarity, to tolerate inconsistencies, and contradictions measured by Budner's *Test of Intolerance of Ambiguity* (Shanker, 1970).

Value Orientation

The administration of the Allport, Vernon, Lindzey Study of Values provides a "scale for measuring the dominant interests in personality" (Allport, Vernon. Lindzey, 1960, p. 1). The instrument is designed to identify Spranger's classification of "Types of Men." Six value orientations are included in this scale prepared in Hindi by Ojha (1976).

Basic Assumptions

Some of the basic assumptions which have been stated and tested in many studies have been taken for granted. For example, first, it is assumed that abilities involved in being creative are universal and that these abilities can be cultivated by adequate procedures. Second, that such abilities are expressed in our daily life, through invention, discovery, curiosity, imagination, experimentation, exploration and the like, as well as their final products, such as scientific inventions, engineering configurations, improved products, designs, paintings and the like. Some other assumptions are as follows:

1. The Purdue Creativity Test is valid and reliable in measuring creativeness and in discriminating between high and low creative subjects.

2. The Culture Fair Intelligence Test provides a valid and reliable measure of intelligence.
3. The Mechanical Reasoning Test is a valid and reliable psycometric device used in measuring understanding of mechanical and physical principles in familiar situations.
4. Ojha's Value Test is a valid and reliable instrument for measuring the relative strengths of the six values as described by Spranger.
5. The Perceptual Simplicity-Complexity Test is valid and reliable in measuring the perceptual preferences.
6. The Budner Tolerance-Intolerance of Ambiguity Scale is a valid and reliable instrument in measuring the tolerance-intolerance of ambiguity.

Hypotheses

Attendent upon and congruent with the objectives stated earlier, the following hypotheses are proposed regarding mechanical reasoning, value orientation, simplicity-complexity and intolerance of ambiguity of the creative individuals;

H_1 There is no significant difference between the high and the low creative subjects on the mechanical reasoning ability which could be regarded as one aspect of intelligence.

H_2 (a) There is no significant difference between the high and low creative individuals in their theoretical value-orientations.

(b) There is no significant difference between the high and the low creative individuals in their economical value-orientations.

(c) There is no significant difference between the high and the low creative individuals in their aesthetic value-orientations.

(d) There is no significant difference between the high and the low creative individuals in their social value-orientations.

(e) There is no significant difference between the high and

the low creative individuals in their political value-orientations.

(f) There is no significant difference between the high and the low creative individuals in their religious value-orientations.

H_3 There is no significant difference between the high and the low creative individuals in their perception for cognitive simplicity and complexity.

H_4 There is no significant difference between the high and the low creative subjects on a measure of intolerance of ambiguity.

Delimitations of the Study

The study was confined to :

(a) Mechanical Engineering students of all the diploma-level engineering institutions for boys in the Union Territory of Delhi.

(b) Students studying in mechanical engineering branch during the session 1977-78.

(c) Students studying in other branches of engineering are beyond the purview of this study.

CHAPTER IV

Engineering Creativity: A Research Perspective

The theoretical approaches to creativity have been discussed in the earlier chapter and an attempt is being made in the present chapter to review researches pertaining to engineering creativity and other variables.

Creativity, as has been pointed out by Taylor (1964), is a large but embryonic field, filled with unknowns. During the last two decades the subject of creativity has received a lot of attention, resulting in a tangle of research reports. The tangle, like all tangles, seems hopelessly confused and complicated. But this confusion is really a tribute to the apparent vigour and progress in creativity research (Repucci, 1971). Almost similar view has been reckoned by Maslow (1972) when he said that the thinking and the research in the field of creativeness tends to be too atomistic and too ad-hoc, and that it is not as holistic, organismic, or systematic, as it could be and should be.

The state of creativity research in India, as elsewhere, is "a mixture of some models, limited applications, operational and non-operational definitions, random speculations, and hypotheses testing" (Roweton, 1973). As has been pointed out by

Mitra (1975) research on creative behaviour in India has started receiving serious attention only very recently. There is, in this country, a lot of slumbering creativity that needs to be liberated and expressed. The creative initiative, the creative vision, and the creative force of the masses remain largely untapped. Unleashing these represents a profound challenge. But challenge, perhaps, is opportunity (Raina, 1976).

There is, however, general agreement at this time (Mitra, 1972 ; Paramesh, 1972) that research activity in the field of creativity must improve in quantity as well as quality.

An advantage of the scantiness of work in the field is that it is possible to break new grounds and understand the dynamics of creativity in our cultural context. A breakdown of Indian research in creativity reveals that the majority of research has been done in the area of personality as related to creativity, while other important areas remain yet to be investigated.

TABLE 2

(1974)

Classification of Indian Research in Creativity in Major Fields

Fields of Research	*No. of Studies*	*Per cent*
Process of creativity	26	34.2
Creativity in relation to personality	29	38.2
Creativity in relation to achievement and other similar variables	7	9.2
Creative environment	6	7.9
Creative product	3	3.9
Miscellaneous	5	6.6
	76	100.0

A subsequent survey (Raina, 1975 d) reveals that one year later, a total of 133 studies were done by Indian researchers and by foreign authors using Indian subjects for their study. A review of the available literature on creativity research in India reveals that most of the studies have been made taking either school students or teachers as the samples. There have been very few studies on professional groups in our social and cultural context. There is hardly any study available on engineering diplomates who constitute a very significant segment of engineering hierarchy. The present study is therefore an endeavour to investigate into this hitherto unexplored professional group which permeates the broad spectrum of occupations lying between the craftsmen on the one hand and the technologist on the other.

Studies on Engineers

A review of researches reported in *A Survey of Research in Psychology* (Mitra, 1972) shows that quite a good number of studies have been conducted in India on the traits of successful and unsuccessful engineering students as well as engineers. Pal (1968 b) has made an elaborate personalistic study of the students of engineering, law, medicine and teacher-trainees and determined their value patterns (Pal, 1967 a), personaiity needs (Pal, 1968 a), and personality adjustment (1968 c). Sinha and Misra (1961 a, 1961 b, 1963) have made a comprehensive study of sociological and psychological factors in success in engineering. Misra (1962) made a study of the non-intellectual factors and success in engineering education. Pestonjee and Akhtar (1969) analysed the occupational value preferences and income aspirations of the engineering students and teacher-trainees, using Centre's Job Value Cards. Gopal (1974) conducted a study of certain differentiating personality variables of creative and non-creative science and engineering students. Akinboye (1981) assessed partners of creativity in budding engineers. Results of this study generally indicated the hierarchy of creativity behaviours manifested by the subjects. Creativity motivation was observed to be basic to all other creativity dimensions. This was followed by fluency, originality and flexibility in that order. Thus : Motivation>Fluency>Originality>Flexibility. But no study has perhaps been reported on creativity in engineers in our cultural context.

Much of the recent research which has been done upon engineering creativity has been aimed at scientists rather than engineers. Little has been done in the way of organised research directly and genuinely relevant to engineering creativity. However, results are available from a number of scattered pieces of work done mostly in the US. No research as yet has been reported in this country on creative behaviour in engineers. After making an extensive survey of creativity in engineering, Blade (1963) recommended that research should be continued on identification of talented and creative students in engineering. Discussing the nature of this quest Leo Rosten (1963) said :

> To unlock the awesome power of the atom was nothing in my judgement compared to what will happen when we mortal men unlock the power of the beauty, the bearing, the infinite imaginativeness which still resides in secret untapped places within the human spirit.

In the light of the above a review of researches is presented in the following pages which explains in general what has been done on the variables chosen for the present study and in particular as related to engineering.

Creativity in Relation to Intelligence

Perhaps the most significant contribution of the last two decades of research on the structure of human abilities is the growing emphasis now given to creativity as a subject for empirical study (Mehdi, 1974). The now-too-well-known researches of Guilford and his associates on the structure of intellect (1950 & 1956) have brought to the fore the existence of two distinct types of thinking abilities, namely convergent thinking and divergent thinking. While the former implies a single already ascertained right response, the latter results in a 'variety of responses involving fluency, flexibility, originality and elaboration'. With the distinction thus made, convergent thinking came to be identified with intelligence as usually defined and measured by the well-known intelligence tests, while divergent thinking gave the most obvious indication of what is generally understood by the term 'creativity'.

While most of the psychologists would agree that there is an important relationship between creativity and intelligence they differ markedly in emphasis. The extent to which 'intelligent' and 'creative' describe independent traits is still hotly debated. Some studies suggest very little overlap, others indicate that the two are virtually indistinguishable. The main means of deciding this question empirically is by the techniques of correlation and factor analysis. Althouah these have been widely employed in the study of creativity and intelligence, results have been conflicting, owing partly to the presuppositions of the investigators and partly to misunderstandings about the strengths and limitation of the techniques.

In real life situations, however, it is noticed that those who make creative contribution to the development of society are not necessarily those who are highly intelligent. Thurstone (1950) in discussing the correlation between intelligence and creativity commented :

> It is commom observation in the universities that those students who have high intelligence, judged by available criteria, are not necessarily the ones who produce the most original ideas. All of us probably know a few men who are both creative and highly intelligent but this combination is not the rule. There is undoubtedly a positive correlation between creative talent and intelligence, so that geniuses are usually in the upper half of the general intelligence distribution.

The suspicion that in most of the standardized intelligence tests the very important domain of intellectual ability, creativity, was being neglected has existed for some time. In 1898 Dearborn observed that some of his more "intellectual" subjects were least imaginative. The same sort of observation was made sporadically by a variety of experimenters in the ensuing twenty years. Simpson in an article several years after the development of psychometrically sophisticated Stanford-Binet intelligence test, was perspicuous enough to write: "Tests . . . to ascertain either native intelligence or acquired knowledge . . . (have) no elements in them to extract from the mind of the individual his powers of creative productivity and his tendencies toward originality".

Much of the recent wave of enthusiasm for the subject had its starting-point in the inaugural address to the American Psychological Association by J.P. Guilford (1950) in which he drew attention to "education's appalling neglect of the study of creativity." In fact much of the experimental work on creativity has been inspired by the pioneering efforts of Guilford and his associates at the University of California who pushed forward basic research work on creative abilities. Guilford's view of intelligence, however, is a special one. Briefly, in his system, intelligence is fragmented into over a hundred independent components or facets (Guilford, 1967), relatively little attention is given to the superordinate, co-ordinating aspects of intelligent behaviour. This fragmentation is so complete, and intelligence, as commonly understood both in popular usage and in view of a large proportion of psychologists, disappears so unequivocally that Guilford's system has sometimes been described by psychologists of a different persuasion as "Hamlet without the Prince of Denmark".

Guilford's three dimensional model entitled 'The Structure of Intellect' presented for the first time empirical evidence in favour of the existence of a set of mental abilities in the structure of intellect that seem to have promise as direct contribution to successful creative thinking. From the results of his investigations, Guilford concluded "we must look well beyond the boundaries of the IQ if we are to fathom the domain of creativity". Rejecting the prevailing doctrine that intelligence is a single, monolethic ability, and also the view that creative talents are something outside the realm of intelligence, the studies through the application of multivariate methods of factor analysis, began with the assumption that there are several, perhaps many, distinguishable

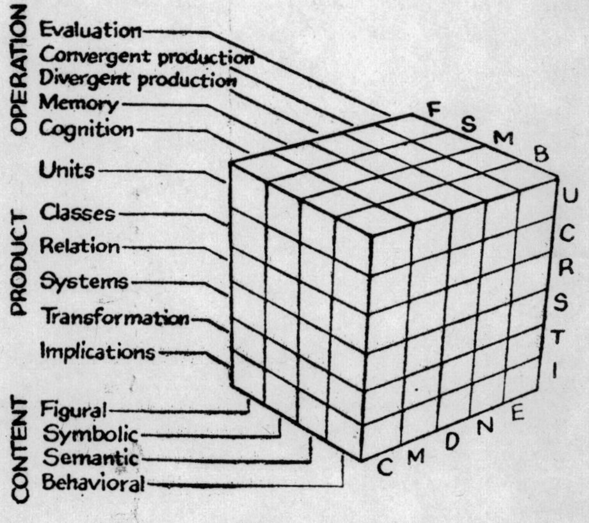

Fig. 1

Theorical Model for the Complete "Structure of Intellect"

abilities involved. Guilford (1950) stated the hypotheses and assumptions that were basic to his theory of 'Structure of Intellect' as :

Creativity represents patterns of primary abilities, patterns which can vary with different spheres of creative ability. Each primary ability is a variable, along which individuals differ in continuous manner. Consequently, the nature of these abilities can be studied in people who are not necessarily distinguished for creative reasons. Productivity depends upon primary traits, including interests, aptitudes and temperamental variables.

Briefly, the abilities believed to be most relevant for creative thinking were identified by Guilford and his associates; they were : (a) Sensitivity to a problem (b) figural spontaneous flexibility; (c) figural adaptive flexibility; (d) word fluency; (e) expressional fluency; (f) semantic spontaneous flexibility; (g) ideation fluency; (h) associational fluency; (i) originality; (j) semantic elaboration; (k) figural redefinition; (l) semantic redefinition; (m) symbolic redefinition. The Structure of Intellect model was represented in terms of three dimensions of operations, products and contents (Guilford and Merrifield, 1960). The model of morphological design includes: five operations or processes (Cognition, memory, divergent thinking, convergent thinking and evaluation), six products (units, classes, relations, systems, transformations and implication) and four contents (figural, symbolic, semantic and behavioural). The greatest potential value of this model, according to Guilford, is that it offers a unified general theory of intelligence.

Since the recognition of the divergent production abilities, the many studies conducted to probe the relationship of creativity and intelligence concern the empirical distinction between them whether or not they are separate domains.

Perhaps the best known research to produce systematic evidence that creativity and intelligence might be independent traits was that of Getzels and Jackson (1962). The results of the study showed, in particular, the 'high creative' children to have a more lively sense of humour, to come from less 'academic' families, to hold less conformist values, and to 'over-achieve' in school work relatively to their IQ. But the generality of these findings is open to some doubt, both because within this special group only contrasting and extreme minorities were studied in detail, and the majority of the children whose performance was not so fully described were neither exceptionally 'creative' nor exceptionally 'intelligent' but scored more or less equally on both sets of tests.

Getzels and Jackson reported correlations between their tests of creativity and also correlations of these tests with IQ. Such correlations, when compared provide crucial evidence as to whether creativity and intelligence can justifiably be considered distinct traits. The evidence in this case was inconclusive. Correlations between tests of creativity were somewhat, but not very markedly, higher than the correlations with IQ. Further examination and analysis by other writers (e.g. Burt, 1962 ; Marsh, 1964) led them to conclude that no convincing separation of creativity from intelligence had been demonstrated.

Rather similar work to that of Getzels and Jackson has been done by Hudson in England who, like Getzels and Jackson, investigated the differing characteristics of the two groups. He found that the differences went beyond cognitive style and seemed to reflect deep variations in personality including differences in type of ego defence mechanism adopted.

Other investigators have reported consonant findings. A correlation of .3 was found by Yamamoto (1964 b) between Torrance Creativity Test scores of creative adolescents and the Lorge-Thorndike measure. Investigating scientifically oriented, bright students, Herr, Moore, and Hansan (1965) did not find any relationship between the Guilford tests of creativity and scores on the Lorge-Thorndike, Watson-Glaser Critical Thinking Appraisal, and Terman Concept Mastery measures. Using seven creativity instruments and taking the Getzels and Jackson study as his starting point, Flescher (1963) reported the average correlation with California Test of mental Maturity scores as .04 for his sample of 110 sixth graders, suggesting definite independence of creativity indices from intelligence. Torrance (1963, 1967) clarifying misinterpretations of the Getzels and

Jackson study (1962) and his own partial replication (Torrance, 1959, 1960, 1962) of it stated, "if we identify a group of children as being either highly intelligent or highly creative, about 30 per cent of them will be both highly intelligent and highly creative."

Hasan and Butcher (1966) produced results quite different from those of Getzels and Jackson. 175 children (100 boys, 75 girls) were tested with a battery of creativity tests. It was found that 'creativity' and 'intelligence' overlapped to such an extent as to be hardly distinguishable.

This failure to separate creativity from intelligence in a representative group of children has been paralleled in American studies. Edwards and Tyler (1965) found almost entirely negative results and concluded that Getzels and Jackson's findings about the relation of creativity, intelligence and school achievement were not widely generalizable.

After reviewing a number of other American studies, and making their careful analysis and evaluation, Wallach and Kogan (1965) concluded that in none of them had creativity been satisfactorily demonstrated to be a unitary trait distinct from intelligence. However, they believed that "creativity had not yet been given a fair chance to reveal as a different form of excellence than intelligence (Wallach and Kogan, 1976).

Although varying conceptions of the meaning of creativity had been embodied in the measures used in previous researches, they all shared one thing in common : they had been administered to persons under study as 'tests'. Such a test-like context was inimical to the wholehearted display of cognitive characteristics which could be correctly referred to as being involved in creativity" (Wallach, Kogan, 1972). With this in mind they formulated a research programme wherein all the psychological measures were obtained in situations designed to minimize 'test anxiety'. When the results of the creativity assessment procedures were compared with results of the intelligence measures, a definite divergence was obtained – the kind that had not been found in earlier studies. Two further facts revealed by this research, which tended to be different from earlier studies were :

the various measures of creativity that were utilized had a great deal in common with one another and that the indices of creativity and the indices of intelligence tended to be independent of each other. The obtained facts did support the view that in school children creativity is a different type of cognitive excellence than general intelligence. The findings of Dentler and Mackler (1964) too support the assumption that pressures of time and evaluation may, indeed, be significant influences in the creativity-intelligence differentiation.

However, a consistent finding of a number of studies probing into the relationship of creativity and intelligence has been that intelligence does not, in and of itself, account for creativity. A certain minimum level of intelligence is generally required—but beyond this level, creativity is accounted for by other factors. Describing creative people Nicholls (1976) stated that creative people must be moderately highly, though not necessarily outstandingly intelligent. In this context, intelligence is best taken to mean competent in the skills and knowledge relevant to the area of work, a view implicit in Kuhn's (1963) suggestion that you have to be a traditionalist before you can be an innovator.

Investigators at the Institute of Personality Assessment and Research (IPAR) provide additional support for the creativity intelligence dichotomy where the creativity dimension was based on ratings. Among artists, correlations between creativity (rated quality of work) and measured intelligence (Terman Concept Mastery Test) were zero or slightly negative (Barron, 1963 a). MacKinnon (1961) provided additional substantiating evidence gathered from creative architects. Within this group, the correlation of intelligence, measured by the Terman Concept Mastery Test, and creativity in architecture as rated by experts, was −.08, which is not significantly different from zero. Even in fields such as mathematics and science where intelligence is a prerequisite for the mastery of the subject matter, the correlation, although positive, was a low .07 (Gough, 1961).

Barron (1963 a) has observed that commitment to creative endeavours is already selective for intelligence, so that the average IQ is already a superior one. Consequently, he has suggested that over the total range of intelligence and creativity, a low, positive correlation of about .4 exists. Beyond the IQ of 120, however, measured intelligence appears to be a negligible factor in creativity. McNemar (1964) appeared to be in agreement with this theory when he stated that "at high IQ levels there will be a very wide range of creativity whereas as we go down to average IQ, and on down to lower levels, the scatter for creativity will be less and less". It is hardly surprising that this "fan shaped" hypothesis, more recently reiterated by Guilford (1967 b), was not confirmed by Mednick and Andrews (1967) and by Ginsberg and Whittemore (1968), who found a positive linear relationship throughout the range.

The IPAR data, along with findings previously cited, appear to provide some evidence for describing creativity as a concept at the same level of abstraction as intelligence. Even Thorndike (1966), who so severely criticized the Getzels and Jackson and Guilford studies, conceded that their data suggested that "there is some reality to a broad domain, distinct from the domain of the conventional intelligence test to which the designation of 'divergent thinking' or 'creative thinking' might be applied". He considered this distinguishable domain rather "nebulous and loosely formed", any different creativity measures being necessarily less interchangeable and equivalent than different intelligence measures. Chambers (1969) has hypothesised that a minimal level of convergent thinking abilities is essential for creative productivity. Beyond this 'floor' there is no relationship between level of convergent thinking abilities and level of creativity. The 'floor' level varies according to the specific dimensions of creativity. The results obtained by Daccy and Madaus (1971) also confirm the contention that the relationship between creativity and intelligence throughout the entire range of IQ is not the same, and have implications for the possibility of thinking in terms of threshold or critical level of IQ beyond which creativity operates independently.

Correlational Studies

Statistical relationship between creativity and IQ depends upon the range of intelligence scores sampled (Ripple and May, 1962). Scores obtained from heterogeneous IQ samples may be more predictive of creative behaviour than intelligence scores from relatively homogeneous samples merely because the increased population variance increases correlations.

On the basis of the analysis of the data reported by Wilson *et al* (1954) and Guilford and Christensen (1956), Thorndike (1963) found that the average correlation among the general intelligence tests was more related among themselves (.43) than the average correlation among the divergent thinking tests (.27). Further, the relationship between intelligence tests and divergent thinking tests was found to be .24. Analysing another set of data of Guilford and his associates, Thorndike pointed out that the mean correlation among the various intelligence tests remained .23, while that among the divergent thinking tests was .14. The correlation between general intelligence and divergent thinking was .12. From these analyses, Thorndike (1963) questioned the possibility of "any common characteristic running through these tests to which the common term creativity may legitimately be applied".

By reanalysing the data of Guilford *et al* (1957), Ward (1966) confirmed the findings of Thorndike (1963) regarding the relationship between creativity and intelligence ; who obtained a correlation of .24 among the convergent thinking tests and a correlation of .18 among the divergent thinking tests. The correlation between the convergent and divergent thinking tests was .15. Cicirelli (1964) found the correlation among the creativity measures as .37 and coefficients of correlation between the creativity and intelligence measures as significant, being in the neighbourhood of .30. Perry (1966) found the correlations between creativity scores on Torrance's test and Intelligence scores obtained on the Otis Mental Ability Tests to be .50. Results confirming this pattern are reported by many researchers (Wodtke, 1964 ; Henderson, 1965). A few studies reporting results contrary to this are also found in literature (Fleming and Weintraub, 1962 ; Edwards and Tyler, 1965). Yamamoto (1964a) administered a battery of creative thinking tests to 272 high school students and identified three groups of "gifted" students in each grade namely High intelligence group, High creativity group and High intelligence-creativity group. When *r*s between IQ and creativity were computed for each grade, it was found that, except in the tenth grade, coefficients were less than .20 and statistically non-significant. In the tenth grade, *r* was .56 and statistically significant. For all 272 *S*s, an *r* of .30 was significant (p—.01) ; *r*s between IQ and creativity in the three "gifted" groups were statistically non-significant. In other words the findings supported the results of previous studies of Getzels and Jackson (1962) and Torrance (1959).

Summarising the correlational information about creativity-Intelligence relationship, Torrance (1967) found that from the total of 178 coefficients of correlation between measures of intelligence and total or composite measure of creativity, the median was .20 ; the median of 88 coefficients between intelligence and verbal creativity was .21, whereas the median of the 114 coefficients of correlations between intelligence and figural creativity was .06. The distributions of product moment coefficients of correlation between scores on intelligence tests and scores on creative thinking tests are presented in Table 3.

Factor Analytic Studies

Cropley (1966) extensively studied an unselected group of children on six measures of 'covergent' thinking and seven of 'divergent' thinking. When the battery was analysed, five apparently significant factors were found which when orthogonally rotated, it proved impossible to obtain a factor of divergent thinking that was not also characterised by high loadings of some convergent measures. Cropley concluded that "It would

TABLE 3

Distributions of Product-Moment Coefficients of Correlation Between Scores on Intelligence Tests and Scores on Creative Thinking Tests*

Coefficient of Correlation	*Total*		*Verbal*		*Figural*	
	Freq.	*Cum. Freq.*	*Freq.*	*Cum. Freq.*	*Freq.*	*Cum. Freq.*
.60 or above	3	3	1	1	0	0
.50 to .59	10	13	2	3	0	0
.40 to .49	13	26	5	8	4	4
.30 to .39	28	54	9	17	3	7
.20 to :29	36	90	30	47	14	21
.10 to .19	33	123	19	66	25	46
.00 to .09	27	150	5	71	29	75
—.01 to —.10	17	167	9	80	26	101
—.11 to —.20	7	174	5	85	8	109
—.21 to —.30	4	178	3	88	4	113
—.31 to —.40	0	178	0	88	1	114
Median	.20		.21		.06	

* **From Torrance, E.P. Minnesota studies of creative behaviour. Georgia : Univ. of Georgia, 1967.**

be wrong to argue either that convergent and divergent thinking cannot be distinguished from each other factorially or that they are completely independent of each other . . . it is unacceptable to think of creativity as a separate basic intellective mode."

In another factorial study of convergent and divergent thinking Lovell and Shields (1967) come to rather similar conclusions. Cropley and Maslany (1969) indicated the existence of large loadings of creativity on intelligence and vice-versa. However, the failure of Cropley and Maslany to establish the independence of creativity assessed by Wallach and Kogan tests from intelligence is attributed by Kogan (1971) to the failure to rotate. A promax rotation of Cropley-Maslany principal components solution by Kogan has yielded pure creativity factor, besides two intelligence factors.

Employing Multiple Group Factor methods Fee (1968) extracted four first and two second order factors. He found the second order factor to differentiate clearly between creativity and intelligence tests although they themselves were slightly correlated. Fee concluded that creativity is clearly not unidimensional.

Creativity-Intelligence Studies with Engineers

For individuals to be creative in engineering, they must generally have an I. Q. of 115 or greater (Gregory, 1972). Buhl (1958) used a group of 167 first-term freshman engineers as subjects in an attempt to identify and understand the creative engineer. The results show a close correlation between creativity and scholastic achievement at the end of the college freshman year. Some correlation was found between creativity and mental ability as measured in the ACE Test. It was pointed out, however, that a high mental potential does not necessarily ensure a high creative ability, even though an individual with a high mental potential has a greater opportunity to exercise his creative ability.

In order to determine the relative effectiveness of the intelligence test as compared with creativity tests, in predicting creative aspects of teaching performance, Chorness and Nottelmann (1956) studied fifty-two Air Force student-instructors. It was found that the course grade tended to be better predicted by creativity test scores than by intelligence test scores, although the differences were not significant.

Owens *et al.* (1957) in a bid to develop and evaluate tests to discriminate creative from non-creative machine designers found, as a result of the experiment, that 'creatives' are not differentiated from 'non-creatives' by general mental ability. They also present evidence that creativity is somewhat 'specific' to the field in question. Owens (1972) reported a follow-up study of 1537 students of 1955 in 1964. This study in the ultimate analysis included 931 *S*s representing R & D engineers, R & D engineers promoted to engineering management and other miscellaneous engineering jobs. The study suggested reasonable independence of creativity from general ability within the present sample; similar to the findings of Getzels and Jackson (1962).

In a longitudinal study of a group of 143 chemical engineers Moffie (1968) concluded that Intelligence was not significantly related to creative managerial performance. The results obtained from this study are comparable to the notion that intelligence is not related to creativity once a given level of intelligence has been reached.

Creativity-Intelligence Studies in India

Few studies in the creativity-intelligence domain have also been reported in India. Gakhar and Kaura (1977) studying 220 girls of mean age 16 years demonstrated an isolation of creativity measures from intelligence. However, a small overlap of two variables was noticed on a factor of 'General Intelligence'.

Rawat and Agarwal (1977) studying 300 *S*s concluded that the high achievers on intelligence are not high achievers on creativity so it is unacceptable to think of creativity as a separate intellective mode.

It is interesting to note, therefore, that whereas now intelligence and creativity are subsumed under wider mental power called 'intellect', the early psychometricians subsumed creativity under intelligence and often tended to depreciate its alleged separate identity. This was true not only of the early unifactorists such as Binet and Terman, but often even of the first multifactorist, Spearman. Few now a days would agree with Spearman, who declared in *Abilities of Man* (1931) : "All creativeness or originality depends solely on education of correlates, and is therefore merely a manifestation of general intelligence; no special creative power exists". There are some individuals who are high in both intelligence and creativity but they are few. Thus intelligence is a stepping stone towards creativity, just as memory is towards intelligence.

Most of the available research supports the hypothesis that creativity is related to better-than-average intelligence in the total population. But, within a given group of practitioners operating at a fairly high level of intelligence, differences in general intelligence provide no significant prediction of difference in creative performances (Steiner, 1962). Wallach and Wing's study (1969) on the creativity-intelligence distinction also suggested that since a wide range of talented accomplishments that society may wish to sustain and nourish are lost to view by a too heavy raliance on intelligence screening measures, we ought to depend upon identification of ideational ability (a concept quite extraneous to intelligence) that is supportive of talented accomplishment as well.

Research Immense but Incomplete

Thus it is surprising to note that, whereas, the extent of research to date is immense in this area it is not complete. Although the general trend of research results about the relationship between creativity and intelligence point to the type of lack of correlation as described by Wallach and Kogan i. e. very high intelligence and creativity are not necessarily positively related, though a somewhat elevated level of intelligence seems crucial—the matter is still in much dispute. Furthermore, 'tests of creativity' not concerned with effect or personality attributes may be an over-simplification and may, perhaps, be tapping a very low level of creativity—reception or differentiation—which may be far afield from the product or performance, and the life activities domain. The inconclusiveness of the results, therefore, seems to suggest that perhaps, until the personological context in which the cognitive variables are embedded is determined, real measures of the dimension of creativity remain elusive.

Creativity in Relation to Mechanical Reasoning

The ability to conceptualize, reason out and understand mechanical and physical principles as applied to a variety of day to day life situations seems to have considerable promise for creative problem-solving in the field of Mechanical Engineering. This ability, as measured by the Mechanical Reasoning Test, may be regarded as one aspect of intelligence, if intelligence is broadly defined (Bennett, 1947).

Presented below is a review of available research which has been attempted to study the creativity mechanical reasoning relationship especially with engineering samples. However, a scanning of the related literature indicates that not many researches have been reported which study this specific relationship.

An extensive study using 103 subjects composed mainly of electronics engineers and scientists (Taylor, 1958) yielded interesting results on the relationship between certain tests and behaviour variables, and creative research work. These men had taken the following tests : the strong Vocational Interest Blank which was scored for the engineering scale, the Terman Concept Mastery Test developed for use with gifted children, the Owen-Bennett Mechanical Comprehension Test, the Test for Productive Thinking, and the Test for Selecting Research Personnel. Following correlations were obtained with the Owen-Bennett Mechanical Comprehension Test when related to the descriptive and Check-list rating form :

	Owen—Bennett Machanical Comprehension Test
Check-List Rating Form	+.29 (.05 significance)
Descriptive Rating Form Quality of Work	+.20
Initiative	+.21
Originality	+.15
Skill-with-people	+.10

While discussing the details of Bennett Test of Mechanical Comprehension Moffie (1968) noted that the Test correlates rather highly with some other tests. Correlations of .45 were obtained using the Otis Intelligence Test and the Bennett Test in an introductory engineering course. Correlations between +.51 and +.44 were obtained when the Revised Minnesota Paper Form Board was related to the Bennett Test (Bennett, 1956). In his own longitudinal study from 1947 to 1951 Moffie (1968) studied 143 chemical engineers with the objective of predicting their creative managerial performance. It was found that mechanical and scientific aptitude, as measured by the Bennett Mechanical Comprehension Test and the Stanford Scientific Aptitude Test, did have some statistically significant relationships with creative performance. These were principally with Stanford Scientific Aptitude Test and five of them did reach the .05 significance level. These relationships were with 'enthusiasm', 'fluency', 'activity', 'flexibility' and 'initiative'. They were all negative correlations. The Bennett Mechanical Comprehension Test correlated significantly with 'activity' on the Rating Form. This correlation was also negative and significant at the .05 level. Thus it was concluded that Mechanical and scientific aptitude although important for college success, show a few significant negative relationships to creative performance.

Owens, Schumacher and Clark (1957) in their study on the measurement of creativity in machine design tried to develop and evaluate tests to discriminate creative from non-creative machine designers. A battery of five instruments was used viz : Power Source Apparatus Test, Application of Mechanisms Test, Personal Inventory and Personal History Form. It was found that 'creatives' are not differentiated from 'non-creatives' by general mental ability. They also present evidence that creativity is somewhat "specific" to the field in question. The study was followed in 1964 for which the potential pool of *S*s consisted of 1537 students of 1955 who were, typically, originally tested as beginning upper class men in the mechanically-related branches of engineering. In the final analysis for the follow up study, however, a total of 931 *S*s were involved: 457 R & D engineers, 104 former R & D engineers promoted to engineering management and 370 working engineering educators, sales engineers and in other miscelleneous job categories. The study arrived at following conclusions :

1. The Power Source Apparatus Test was found to be a better predictor of creativity in machine design than a well-regarded mental ability or scholastic aptitude test.
2. Prediction of creativity is enhanced by appraising not only cognitive characteristics, but non-cognitive and environmental characteristics as well.

The report *Variables Related to Creativity and Productivity among Men in Two Research Laboratories* (Taylor, 1953) presents two studies designed to explore the relation of certain tests and other variables to the creativity and productivity of men engaged in research and developmental work. The *S*s, composed mainly of electronics and scientists, were administered a series of five tests including those of Form CC of the Mechanical Comprehension Test, Test of Productive Thinking and

Test for Selecting Research Personnel. An analysis of the data revealed significant correlations between each of these three tests.

Lawshe and Harris (1960) correlated flexibility, fluency and total scores obtained on the Purdue Creativity Test with the Wonderlic Personnel Test—a test of mental alertness, and the Mechanical Comprehension Test Form CC. The product-moment correlations are presented in the following Table.

TABLE 4

Correlations Between Creativity Scores and Other Tests

	Wonderlic $N=48$	*Mechanical Comp (CC)* $N=43$
Fluency	.15	—.08
Flexibility	.15	.13
Total score	.16	—.01

The correlations indicated that the creativity scores were not measuring the same abilities as these other two tests.

In his study designed to develop and validate a creative ability test for surveying the technical supervisory personnel of an industrial concern Harris (1955) used ten tests which included among others tests of Mathematical Reasoning and General Reasoning. A group of 32 supervisory and engineering personnel were selected for preliminary testing. As a result five tests including that of Mathematical Reasoning were eliminated because of the lack of variability in scores. The remaining tests along with that of General Reasoning were then grouped to from a combined test. The combined test correlated highly with supervisory judgments of performance of the seven independent samples of individuals used. These included engineers, engineering students, technical personnel and hourly employees.

Attempting to identify and understand the creative engineer, differentiating the highly creative individuals from the less creative ones and determining the attributes which appear pertinent to creativity, Buhl (1958) in his study showed a close correlation between creativity and scholastic achievement at the end of the college freshman year. Some relationship was found between creativity and mental ability as measured in the ACE Test.

Irvine (1968) made a study of the relationship of creative thinking ability to psychomotor ability, mechanical reasoning ability and vocational attitude of selected high school arts students. An investigation into this relationship between creative thinking and mechanical reasoning was also attempted to by Frantz (1964) in his unpublished master's thesis with eighth grade students as his subjects.

Thus it will be seen from the above studies that creativity in a specialized field requires in addition to motivational or personological qualities, specific qualities of competence in the relevant work, an involvement in it and a sensitivity to its requirements.

Creativity in Relation to Values

Value orientation of the creative individual has been one of the major areas of interest in the field of creativity-personality relationship. A number of investigations have identified certain consistent relationship to exist between creativity and values (Mackinnon, 1962; Barron, 1965).

MacKinnon (1963) using Allport-Vernon-Lindzey Scale of Values with creative architects, research scientists, and mathematicians, indicated that these subjects showed a high elevation on both theoretical and aesthetic values. The highest value according to him, for research scientist is theoretical (57.0) followed by aesthetic (47.5); for architects the aesthetic value is the highest (56.2) with theoretical value in second place (50.8), while for the creative mathematicians the two values, still above average, are approximately equally high-aesthetic (52.9); theoretical (52.0), the strength of political value in general being slightly below average, and the religious, social and economic value following considerably lower. MacKinnon and his research team, reports Torrance (1962), had not anticipated that just these two values

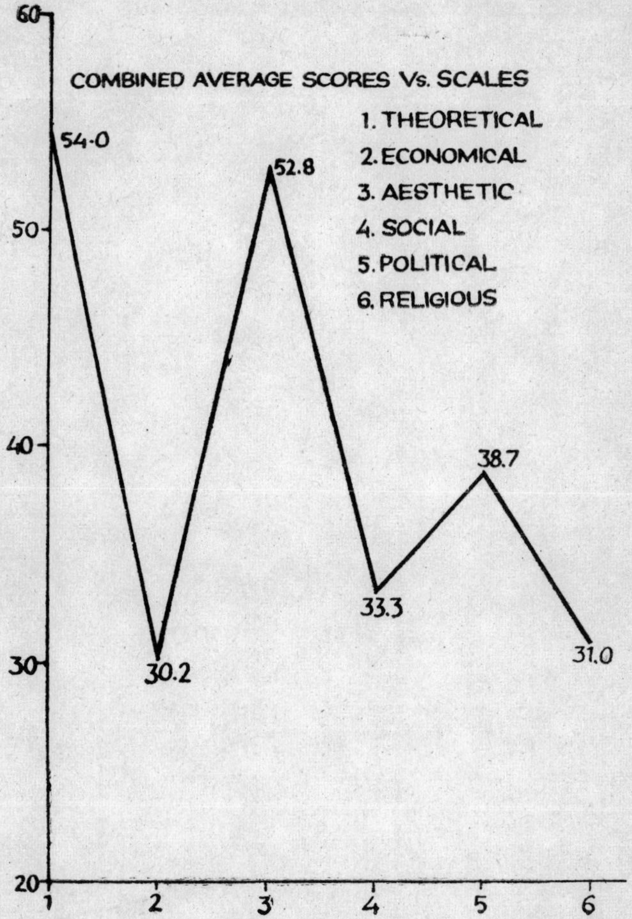

60
50
40
30
20
COMBINED AVERAGE SCORES Vs. SCALES
1. THEORETICAL
2. ECONOMICAL
3. AESTHETIC
4. SOCIAL
5. POLITICAL
6. RELIGIOUS
54·0
52.8
30.2
33.3
38.7
31.0
1
2
3
4
5
6

Chart 1

would be high and of so nearly the same strength for all groups. The authors of the instrument had pointed out that the "aesthetic attitude is in a sense diametrically opposed to the theoretical". MacKinnon explains this contradiction in the creative personality: "if there is a conflict between the theoretical value with its cognitive and rational concern with truth and aesthetic value with its emotional concern with form and beauty, the creative person appears to have the capacity to tolerate the tension that strong opposing values create in him, and in his creative striving he effects some reconciliation of them. It is not sufficient for him that problems are solved; he demands that his solutions be elegant. He seeks both truth and beauty".

AVL study of values was also used by Heist (1968) who observed that his subjects scored very high on the Theoretical and Aesthetic Scales and low on Economic, Religious and Social Scales. The pattern for the combined average scores across several of the available creative profiles of potentially creative groups, as identified by peers and faculty, is as shown in Figure 2 (Heist, 1968) :

The researches by MacKinnon, Gumeson. Walburg and Welch have identified the same profile pattern and "has come to be respected as indicative of atypical, unusual persons."

MacKinnon (1961) reported that on the *California Psychological Inventory*, highly creative architects rated high on aesthetic and theoretical scales and their assertiveness and independence were again graphically displayed on IPAR scales measuring these variables.

In a study on the personality inventory correlates of creativity among architects Hall and MacKinnon (1969) conducted multiple stepwise correlation analyses on each of seven personality inventories, one of them being Allport, Vernon, Lindzey (1951) study of values (AVL). Among MacKinnon's creative architects, 'aesthetic values' were highest with 'theoretical values' almost as high.

These findings of MacKinnon are interesting and thoroughly based. They cry out for repetitions (and for extension to other professional groups) in this country.

Eiduson (1957; 1958) has adduced evidence to show that creative artists have more theoretical and abstract interests. Eiduson (1962) also studies creative scientists who were found to have among other traits, deep seated concern for intellectual activities. Similar results of intellectual orientation towards the outward world among creatives has been reported by Myden (1959) and Reid *et. al.* (1959) who have found creative individuals to tend to value intellectual attainment.

Paramesh (1972) studying 216 adolescents on a scale of values based on Allport, Vernon and Lindzey study of values (1960 a, 1960 b) found high-creative individuals to be significantly higher on theoretical and aesthetic values as compared to the low-creative individuals. In another study to explore the personality of intellectually gifted freshmen as compared to an unselected group of students Warren and Heist (1960) used an Omnibus Personality Inventory and the Allport-Vernon-Lindzey study of values. It was found that the gifted group had greater preference for intellectual activity of a reflective and abstract nature and a stronger aesthetic orientation, especially among the women.

Welsh (1977) administered AVL (Allport, Vernon and Lindzey, 1970) to highly gifted and talented adolescent attending the Governor's School of North Carolina. Correlations of six AVL Values with the five research variables are given in Table 5. Of particular interest are the AVL theoretical (T) and aesthetic (A) scales, since their relationship to creativity in adults has already been demonstrated as stated above (MacKinnon, 1962). Although the correlational patterns are not completely consistent, the general trend is for theoretical values to be positively correlated with intelligence and intellectence and negatively correlated with the Art Scale and Origence. Aesthetic values are positively correlated with intellectence, the Art Scale and Origence, but with somewhat mixed results for the intelligence tests. A pattern of generally negative correlation is found for economic (E), Social (S), and Religious (R) values, and a mixed pattern of relatively low correlations for Political (P) values.

One of the implications of the origence/intellectence persona-

TABLE 5

Correlation of AVL Values with Intelligence Tests, (CMT, D-48), Intellectence Art Scale (RA), and Origence (ORIG)*

AVL Values	*Boys*					*Girls*				
	N=349 CMT	N=170 D-48	N=344 INT	N=349 RA	N=344 ORIG	N=406 CMT	N=193 D-48	N=391 INT	N=402 RA	N=391 ORIG
Theoretical	.23	(.13)	.34	—.15	—.13	.14	.14	.29	(.03)	—.10
Economic	—.18	(.00)	—.24	—.12	—.19	—.17	(—.05)	—.20	(—.07)	—.12
Aesthetic	(.05)	(—.02)	.10	.31	.54	.19	(—.04)	.25	.18	.43
Social	(—.07)	(—.12)	—.09	(.01)	(—.02)	—.11	(—.04)	—.18	—.12	—.16
Political	.10	(.09)	.13	(—.06)	(—.08)	(—.02)	(—.03)	(—.01)	.14	.21
Religious	—.14	(—.09)	—.25	(—.08)	—.26	(—.07)	(.02)	—.20	—.14	—.25

*(r) signifies correlation not significantly different from zero at the .05 Level of confidence.

lity model is that characteristics at the high ends of both dimensions are related to creativity. Evidence has been adduced that this is true for creative architects and possibly for scientists (Welsh, 1975). It is clear from the results as shown in Table 6 that most of the subjects had peak scores on theoretical and aesthetic values, with boys about equally divided between the two but with girls showing twice as many peaks on aesthetic as on theoretical.

TABLE 6

Peak Scores on AVL Value Scales for Subjects in Novant 2, High Origence/High Intellectence

AVL Scales	*Boys*	*Girls*	*Total*	*Percentage*
Theoretical	15	10	25	30.9
Economic	1	0	1	1.2
Aesthetic	16	22*	38	46.9
Social	1	2	3	3.7
Political	1	3	4	4.9
Religious	4	6*	10	12.3
Total	38	43	81	99.9

*Two girls tied on A and R counted as .5 for each Scale.

For boys, of the four cases with peaks on R, two were highest on A and one on T. For girls aesthetic was next highest for one of the two cases with a peak on S, for two of the three P peaks, and for three of the R peaks. Adding these second-highest cases to those with peak scores gives a total of thirty-four boys and thirty-eight girls who have either T or A values of the first or second highest value in the AVL Profile. That is, seventy-two out of eighty-one subjects high on origence and intellectence—88.9 percent—were high on theoretical or aesthetic values.

Finally, a count of those high on both values was made. There were three boys and four girls with theoretical first and aesthetic second, and six boys and four girls had A/T patterns. Thus, while these patterns may be infrequent in gifted adolescent groups, 21.0 percent of the Governor's School subjects who were high on origence and intellectence were also high on both theoretical and aesthetic values. By contrast, only 3.4 percent of eighty-seven students low on both dimensions showed this value pattern, with one additional subject having a tie score on the economic value.

Thus the study concluded that the AVL, intelligence and intellectence seem to be associated primarily with theoretical values, although there is some relation to aesthetic value as well. For many of these *S*s a pattern of aesthetic/theoretical or theoretical/aesthetic values was found.

The studies reviewed above indicate that the need for quality and excellence is a vital ingredient in high level creativity. The creative person seeks to do things in certain ways, and with certain end-results, that he himself considers to be excellent (Chambers, 1969). Maddi (1965) pointed out in this context that D.H. Lawrence rewrote "The Rainbow" eight times, and Clifford (1958) in his study of creative chemists and mathematicians spoke of his *S*'s striving not just for answers to problems but elegance in their work. Thus the foregoing researches bring out a general agreement with MacKinnon and associates' conclusion that highly creative groups tend to get relatively high scores on both theoretical and aesthetic values. This was, rather, a peculiar finding because the authors of AVL regarded the two scales to be antithetical. MacKinnon offered the following interpretation of this rather peculiar finding. The sources of creativity lie in individual's ability to tolerate the tensions generated by the antithetical values and to bring about their synthesis and reconciliation. If an architect's designs are to give delight, the architect must be an artist; if they are to be technologically sound and efficiently planned he must also be something of a scientist, at least an applied scientist or engineer (MacKinnon, 1962 b).

Apart from the studies on theoretical/aesthetic pattern of values research results are also available concerning other four values on the AVL scale of values. Blatt and Stein (1957) studied industrial research chemists and found that the more creative group had higher economic and aesthetic values and lower social, religious, and authoritarian values as compared to their less creative counterparts.

While a study of creative teachers on certain personality variables (Yamamoto, 1963) showed no difference between high and low creativity groups on aestheticism scale; a comparison of a group of innovative Physics teachers with unselected high school teachers on certain personality variables (Walberg and Welch, 1967) indicated the innovatives to be higher on theoretical and aesthetic values and lower on economic, religious and political values, than their non-innovative counterparts. However, Buel and Bachner (1961) investigating research personnel with a set of psychometric instruments in relation to three criteria of creativity found no relationship between most of the personality traits, including values, and creativity.

Paramesh (1970) studied the value orientations of a sample of high school white American students. Results from the creativity measure based on Barron Welsh RA scale and the AVL study of values showed that the high creative group scored significantly low on economic value alone, while no difference was observed on other values among the criterion groups.

Using peer rating as criterion of creativity, Barron (1953 a, 1953 b) found that the creative individuals chosen on this criterion were characterised by aesthetic disposition, among other psychological traits. Windholz (1968) also arrived at similar result of higher level of literary interest and aesthetic experience to be associated with higher levels of creativity. A greater social participation, interest in helping others, and valuing of people too was found to be related to higher level of creativity. Chambers (1972) reports that facilitating teachers self-reported themselves as more aesthetical sensitive than did the inhibiting teachers.

Getzels and Csikszentimihalyi (1964, 1965) reported that on the AVL art students expressed more interest in "aesthetic values" than in "economic" and "social values". Comparing two groups of children—highly intelligent *S*s who were not highly creative, and highly creative *S*s without high IQs—Getzels and Jackson (Getzels and Jackson, 1958, 1961, 1962) found that while both the groups attained similar scholastic achievement, they differed substantially on value orientations (Getzels & Jackson, 1962).

Creativity-Values Studies on Scientists

Studies made on scientists investigating into their value patterns reveal some interesting results. In her intensive investigation of the life histories of 22 eminent physical scientists Roe (1951, 1953, 1956) found them exhibiting little interest in religion or in church-related activities. However, she noted that this indifference was not necessarily a reflection of antagonistic feelings toward religion. This finding has been further substantiated by Terman (1954, 1955) in a well known longitudinal investigation of scientists and non-scientists in a group of approximately 800 gifted men. Reiterating these findings of Roe and Terman, McClelland (1962) has also reported lack of interest in religion among experimental physical scientists. Data on Crutchfield conformity experiment (Chambers, 1972) showed rather similar results viz : on AVL the scientists are notably low in religious, social and economic values.

Creativity-Values Studies on Engineers

There are very few studies on value orientations of engineers as such. However, some studies have been reported regarding the value pattern of engineers taking science students as the *S*s. Studying 504 honours winners in the Science Talent Search, MacCurdy (1961) concluded that the potential engineer was a socially oriented person who enjoyed working with other people, liked to work with his hands, and felt that science was for man's use. He derived much satisfaction, encouragement and help from his family and associates and from publications.

A study of 286 male engineering and applied science freshmen indicated values to be the only variable which showed interaction with ability, it discriminated between achievement levels of the high ability group, but failed to show a relationship with achievement on the other two ability levels. A correlation of .53 between values and grades was obtained for the upper ability group indicating that intrinsic values were characteristic of high achievers and extrinsic values were characteristic of low achievers in that group.

Indian Studies on Creativity in Relation to Values

Review of the available literature shows that very few studies have been conducted in the Indian settings to investigate into the value orientations or value patterns of creative individuals. In one such study concerning personality traits of high creative children, Goyal (1972) concluded that they have a capacity to entertain opposing values. The results of another study by Paramesh (1972) on 216 adolescents indicated that the High-Creative individvals were significantly higher than their Low-Creative counterparts on theoretical and aesthetic value. Girijesh Kumar (1978) in a study on creativity in relation to values in school going adolescents also found that the high creatives possessed a significantly higher degree of theoretical value. The study of Jha (1978) sought to explore and analyze certain personality dimensions relevant to creativity. The findings of this study again indicated that the creative persons were aesthetic in taste. Mallappa and Upadhyaya (1977) found 'social awareness' among their high creative group.

It will be seen from the studies reviewed in this section that research evidences regarding the value orientation of creative engineers are scanty. The situation is none-too-happy in India where little research appears to have been carried out regarding the relationship between creativity and value orientations. Whatever is known about this relationship is mainly due to

American psychologists of the IPAR group. However, the importance of these studies lies in the fact that they have paved the way for further investigations into this important but relatively less explored field.

Creativity in Relation to Simplicity-Complexity

Individual differences in ways of perceiving have been a topic of study for some time but only since the second world war it has been recognised that the perceptual style of an individual is closely related to his personality (Steinberg ; 1964, 1967). Since then a wide variety of research (Barron, 1963 ; Eisenman, 1959 ; Schorder, Driver and Streufert, 1967 ; Schaefer, 1969 ; Raychaudhuri, 1966) has shown that one of the stylistic variables particularly distinctive of the creative is a cognitive preference for complexity - the rich, dynamic, and asymmetrical - as opposed to simplicity. This perceptual style of cognitive complexity is not limited to any particular group of creative subjects but is typical of the creator in almost all fields. Using Revised Art (RA) Scale of the Welsh Figure Preference Test (WFPT), that successfully discriminated between artists and non-artists in standardization and cross-validation sample (Barrón, 1953 ; Barron and Welsh, 1952). Gough (1961) demonstrated this cognitive disposition as characteristic of research scientists, MacKinnon (1961) of creative architects, and Barron (1963) of creative writers. Although different investigators used different measures of complexity-simplicity dimension, nevertheless, as Eisenman and Schussel (1970) observe, despite the different measures utilized, the results are generally consistent with the belief that complexity-simplicity is an important aspect of creativity.

In his large scale investigation with 721 members of the freshman class at MIT, Snyder (1967) using an operational definition of creativity based on the use of three scales : Thinking Introversion Scale, Complexity Scale, Impulse Expression Scale, derived from the Omnibus Personality Inventory concluded that MIT was loosing three times as many students who, when freshman, preferred to investigate 'new solutions' and to take intellectual risks, as those students who preferred a well ordered and regulated life with tangible results.

MacKinnon and Barron have described psychological richness and complexity as one of the attributes of creative person. This perceptiveness of the creative and his openness to richness and complexity of experience is strikingly revealed on the Barron-Welsh Art Scale of the Welsh Figure Performance Test. Some 80 painters in the original study of Barron and Welsh, (1952) showed a marked preference for the complex and asymmetrical, or, as they often referred to them, the vital and dynamic figures. A contrasting sample of nonartists revealed a marked preference for the simple and symmetrical drawings. On the Barron-Welsh Art Scale, the more original scientists differed from the less original ones in preferring the complex asymmetrical figures that artists too prefer (Barron, 1969).

Bulk of the research in this area has come from IPAR studies ; especially those done by Barron, Welsh and MacKinnon. In all the creative groups studied, MacKinnon (1962) found a clear preference for the complex and asymmetrical—in general the more creative a person is the stronger is this preference. Similarly, in several other samples at the IPAR, scores on an Institute Scale measuring preference for perceptual complexity, were significantly correlated with creativity. In the sample of architects the correlation was +0.48. Studying complexity-simplicity as a personality variable Barron (1953) obtained correlations of complexity with variables like Personal Tempo, Verbal Fluency and Constriction as .50, .29 and —.42 respectively. He further concluded that the complex person is more intensely expressive, expansive and fluent in speech than the simple person. The simple person, on the other hand, is seen as being more natural and likeable, and as more straightforward and lacking in duplicity (Complexity correlates —.44 with Naturalness, —.27 with Likeability, and +.56 with Deceitfulness, as rated by the staff). The study clearly revealed the preference for complexity being associated with originality, artistic expression and excellence of aesthetic judgment. The person is seen as more original—correlation with the criterion ratings or originality being .30. The author also stated that originality and artistic creativeness and discrimination were related to the preference for complexity, and that the latter had some relationship to sentience and feminity in men. The complex person's greater flexibility in thought processes is shown by a correlation of —.35 with rated Rigidity. A 22 item scale for Rigidity, developed by Gough and Sanford, yielded an *r* of —.18 with complexity.

The person who prefers complexity is socially non-conformist. With another sample of over 100 male undergraduates Barron (1953) found preference for simplicity to be associated with social conformity, respect for custom and ceremony, friendliness towards tradition, somewhat categorical moral judgment, an undeviating patriotism, and suppression of such troublesome new forces as inventions which would temporarily cause unemployment. Complexity on the other hand was found to be related :

(a) positively to personal tempo, verbal fluency, impulsiveness and expansiveness ;
(b) positively to originality ;
(c) positively to aesthetic interest ;
(d) negatively to rigidity ;
(e) negatively to political-economic conservatism, to subservience, to authority, to ethnocentrism, and to social conformity.

Findings of undeviating patriotism and preference for team effort to individual competition in simple persons have also been reported by Levinson and Sanford (1944) and Welsh (1949).

Barron (1954) studying 343 military officers found a positive relationship between originality and scope-and-complexity as a person. The findings of another study (Barron, 1955) with 100 Air Force captains showed originality to be related to preference for complexity in phenomena.

Preference for complexity is also motivational. A number of studies using the Barron-Welsh Art Scale (Golann, 1962 ;

Helson & Crutchfield, 1970 b) suggest that creative people are relatively higher than controls in preference for complexity. Barron (1958) argues that creative people seek complexity and disorder rather than simplicity and order ; and complex, disordered situations allow the possibility of new orderings and creative products more than do ordered situations.

Investigators employing the "Revised Art Scale" of Welsh Figure Preference Test (RA—WFPT) Welsh, (1959) have shown that the perceptual choice of the artistically disposed are characterized by a preference for asymmetrical, highly complex, irregular, relatively open and freehand designs and a corresponding dislike for geometrical, ruled, closed, relatively simple and apparently balanced figures (Barron & Welsh, 1952 ; Raychaudhari, 1962, 1963, 1965 b ; Welsh, 1959).

In three groups of eminent individuals—Creative writers, mathematicians and architects—it was found that majority of the creative writers, mathematicians and architects—were perceptive type. For architects, preference for perception correlated .41 with rated creativity (Barron, 1969). Another finding of significance is that creative individuals, whether artists, scientists, architects or writers preferred the same kinds of figures that the painters in the original standardization group preferred.

37 Irish managers (Barron ; 1969, 1972) were found to be about half a standard deviation above the general population mean on the Complexity of Outlook Scale. Barron (1970) studied the role of heredity in creativity using the classical twin method. *S*s consisted of 59 pairs of like sexed twins and 29 dizygotic pairs. The average age of the sample was 17. It was found, on the Barron-Welsh Art Scale having highest loading on the factor of "preference for complexity", that the correlation in monozygotic (identical) group is .58 and in the dizygotic (fraternal) group is .07. However, the author could not conclude clearly on the basis of high heritability component ($h^2 = .55$) whether what is inherited is a preference for complexity or a great ability to discriminate in the aesthetic realm.

As part of their research at the IPAR, Crutchfield (1961) reported that creative individuals prefer complexity, that is, they have a strong desire to turn disorder into meaning, to accept innovation and the challenge presented by apparent imperfection.

Apart from the studies emanating from the IPAR group of researchers the variable of simplicity-complexity has attracted the attention of other researchers as well. Callister (1970) investigated individual differences in preference for complexity or simplicity. In this study the tests for degree of complexity-preference seemed to provide a valuable indicator of creative temperament in that the 'high complexity preferring' subjects possessed many of the characteristics commonly found in other studies to be associated with creativity, although they were not superior in intelligence. This study also confirmed the general pattern of validity of the complexity-preference approach and its results showed the descending order in extent of complexity preferred as : arts students, psychologists, engineers.

Schaefer (1969) investigating into the self-image of 800 high school students found that the self-concept of creative adolescents, regardless of sex speciality differences, included such themes as complexity, reconciliation of opposites, impulsiveness and craving for novelty. Eisenmen and Robinson (1967) also had high school students as subjects for measuring this variable using polygons of varying degree of complexity. They found that a preference for complexity in polygons was significantly related to a high score on a paper-and-pencil personality measure of creativity. They reported lack of a significant correlation value (.14) between the Stanford-Binet and the polygon test or creativity test scores also suggested that this dimension was independent of the IQ domain. Evidence pointing toward the early development of this characteristics emerged in Rosen's (1955) investigation of art students. Scores on the Revised Art Scale did not increase as a function of training in art—the scores of the first-year art students not differing significantly from those of the advanced.

Williams (1964) pointed out that apart from the intellectual characteristics there are some very well defined motivational characteristics of scientific and engineering creativity which include among others, preference for complexity. It has been substantiated by Owens (1969, 1972) who concluded on the basis of a longitudinal study of 1537 mechanical engineering students that creative individuals were cognitively complex and that they could integrate more inputs than their less creative fellows :

Buel (1961) obtained 900 definitions of creativity from a group of scientists ; the supervisors of these scientists then rated them on creativity using their own definitions of creativity. These creativity criteria ratings correlated with expressing desire to work on complex problems (+.55).

An important issue, emerging from the study of 185 *S*s (Raychaudhuri, 1966) suggested an examination of the very nature of perceptual preference-pattern as an attribute of personality. A state of perceptual tension between apparently opposing and diametrical forms, ideas, shapes or cues induces a sense of equivocality and complexity in the phenomena (Graves, 1951) seemed pleasurable and gratifying to the artistic person owing to the appropriate imbalance and resulting tension that is desired by his personality system.

Raychaudhuri (1966 b) using the Revised Art (RA) Scale of the Welsh Figure Preference Test furnished supporting cross-cultural evidence. Investigating musicians and painters, he reported that the mean RA scores of these artists were significantly higher than those of non-artists : these obtained differences were reinforced by the findings of another, comparable study (Raychaudhuri, 1966).

Thus it may be concluded from the studies reviewed in this section that creative persons are especially disposed to admit complexity and even disorder into their perceptions without being made anxious by the resulting chaos. It is not so much that they like disorder per se, but that they prefer the richness of the disordered to the stark barrenness of the simple. Developing a multidimensional theory of creativity Chambers (1969) observed that a strong ego, a preference for complexity, aesthetic sensitivity and flexibility in thinking, are all essential traits for creative work regardless of level, field or type.

Creativity in Relation to Intolerance of Ambiguity

Frenkel-Brunswik proposed that some people find it difficult to tolerate or manage ambiguities, inconsistencies or surprises. Such people have a generalized tendency to dichotomize the world ; things and people are seen as all good or all bad ; the world is black or white. When faced with an ambiguous situation, they quickly fix on one concrete interpretation. This way of managing ambiguous situations is found to characterize much of their behaviour and their cognitions of persons and objects, their interpersonal relations and their ways of coping with problems. People who are intolerant of ambiguity are relatively "closed" to new information which would increase the richness of their intellectual resources. Their cognitive palette contains only blacks and whites. Intolerant of ambiguity, they seek simplified good evil solutions to complex social, political and economic issues. In contrast, an open-minded person tries to perceive a situation, however vague it may be, in terms of the objective characteristics of the situation itself rather than in terms of certain preconceived notions and subjectively recognized categories. He prefers, therefore, to postpone his judgment, or tolerate ambiguity of the situation till such time as is required to understand the situation in terms of objective characteristics inherent in the situation itself rather than in terms of ready-made concepts and subjectively recognized categories, which may be irrelevant to the understanding of the situation as it objectively stands.

Hence the tolerance of ambiguity may be defined as the ability to accept conflict and tension resulting from polarity (Fromm, 1959), to tolerate inconsistencies and contradictions (Maslow, 1962), to accept the unknown, to be comfortable with the ambiguous, approximate, uncertain. The creative persons can postpone decisions and accept abeyance as pleasantly challenging. Zilboorg (1959), Wilson (1954), and Hart (1950) concur in this analysis. The ability to tolerate ambiguity appears also related with two other aspects. One is the ability to toy with ideas, rather play-fully rearranging them into different forms. The other is preference for complexity, found by Barron (1963) in his study of artists.

The intolerance of ambiguity is of particular importance to creative functioning as it introduces 'autistic' thinking, an activity which takes such forms as fantasy, wishful thinking, reverie and day-dreaming. It is within the context of 'autistic thinking' that traits like needs, interests and attitudes are expressed which are important factors in the development of creativity. There has been a considerable amount of research dedicated to this aspect of psychological enquiry and this has an important bearing on creativity. In general this research tends to identify the 'inhibitors' to creative thinking, although some writers have shown how it may contribute to the study of the origin and genesis of ideas and their development. Some of the more important papers in this research area are reviewed below.

Snyder (1967) in a substantial article in *Universities Quarterly* examined the effect of 'the institution, the college curriculum and setting', on the development of creativity. He suggested that students in some particular educational disciplines and fields of study may need greater freedom to give time to intellectual risk-taking and to "playing with ideas". "The need for closure, for making a commitment to one of several possible solutions, may be a more crucial experience in the undergraduate education of engineers than in the education of scientists. The student scientist may have and need greater sanction and freedom for intellectual risk-taking than his engineer counterpart. This at least raises the interesting possibility that creative solutions or formulations by engineers may involve 'intolerance' rather than 'tolerance' for ambiguity.

Applying the Myers-Briggs Type Indicator, MacKinnon (1961) determined that a preference for perceptual openness differentiated more creative from less creative architects. The extensive testing programme revealed that creative architects are characterised by dominance, rather low sociability, freedom from conventional restraints and inhibitions, readiness to admit views that were unusual and unconventional. They are more open and receptive to all experience both from within and from without (MacKinnon, 1962). One of the most consistent findings from the IPAR studies is the preference of highly creative subjects for visual material which is apparently lacking in order, complex, asymmetrical, and not organised along stereotyped lines.

In a major study on the personality inventory correlates of creativity among architects Hall and MacKinnon (1968) have produced further evidence on the validity and importance of this measure. They found in creative architects, a decided preference for openness and receptivity, both to experience and new ideas, as well as for a concern with deeper meanings and possibilities inherent in things and situations.

Barron (1958) reported on his investigations of creativity by studying ways in which creative persons differed from others in their responses to order and disorder. He found that the creatives tolerated disorder better and were more able to find unity in disorder in drawings than were others.

From such considerations Barron (Taylor, 1955) developed five hypotheses with regard to creative persons : (1) that they prefer complexity and some degree of apparent imbalance in phenomena, (2) that they are more complex psychodynamically and have greater personal scope (3) that they are more independent in their judgment (4) that they are more self-assertive and dominant, and (5) that they reject suppression as a mechanism for the control of impulse.

Guilford (1959) also reported original person to be more confident and tolerant of ambiguity. Lindgren and Lindgren (1965) submitted evidence that creative undergraduates, selected by the Asymmetrical Preference Test, perceived themselves as a social and "Ornery". McDermid (1964) found his more creative engineers to be high on autonomy, aggression and dominance.

Analyzing biographical data of 132 research personnel, Buel (1965) found that the more creative reacts positively to challenge, seeks unstructured work situations, and desires contemplative pursuits. Therefore, the creative individual's "exceptionally strong need to find order where none appears" may be considered a motivating factor (Barron, 1963 b).

The finding that greater tolerance of ambiguity is shown by relatively more creative Ss has further been substantiated by Stein Morris and Bernard (1954) in their study designed to test the differences in responses to ambiguous stimuli in a group of creative research chemists. Eighteen research chemists were individually rated for creativity by their superiors and colleagues. Each subject was tested on a series of ten standard Rorschach cards exposed in a tachistoscope at four different exposure levels in order to vary the ambiguity of the stimuli. Analysis of the results showed that the more creative chemists responded with greater number of hypotheses as well as a greater number of well-integrated responses (significant at the .01 level) under varying conditions of ambiguity.

Getzels and Jackson (1969) found from their research directed toward discovering significant variable differentiating the creative from the intelligent person that the two experimental groups—one highly creative and other highly intelligent—differed significantly in their fantasy responses. The creative group made greater use of stimulus-free themes, unexpected endings, humour, incongruities and playfulness (Table 7).

TABLE 7

Categories of Fantasy Production of Highly Creative and Highly Intelligent Groups

Content-Analysis Categories	*Group*				
	High Creativity (N=24)		*High IQ (N=28)*		
	Frequency	*Percent*	*Frequency*	*Percent*	x^2
1	2	3	4	5	6
Stimulus-free theme	18	75	11	39	5.31
Unexpected ending	22	92	17	61	5.05
Presence of incongruity	17	71	10	36	5.06

Gust's (1964) study of creative individuals based on high-low scores obtained on Torrance Test of Creativity again culminated in the same finding that the high creative had a better capacity to tolerate tension arising from succurance and nurturance. He possessed the ability to subordinate feelings and conflicts. He was less interested in the empirical, critical and rational and was not aiming to order or systematic knowledge and was not interested in occupations that might involve directing someone, or in following organised plans without significant deviations.

Maslow cited artistic creation, involving the artist, 'to bring together clashing colours, forms that fight each other, dissonances of all kinds into unity' as illustration of resolution of dichotomies in self-actualization. In an effort to identify the particular personality traits which make for creativity, Maslow (1962) presents an extensive list ; the creative personality, he says, is spontaneous, expressive, effortless, innocent, unfrightened by the unknown or the ambiguous, able to accept tentativeness and uncertainty, able to tolerate bipolarity, able to integrate opposites. Hallman (1963, 1967) too has included tolerance of ambiguity within the conditions necessary and sufficient for creativity. He maintains :

> "It is obvious that anyone who tolerates uncertainties and conflicts for long must enjoy an anchorage within some value system apart from the conventional order, and this would need to be himself."

Indian Studies on Creativity-Intolerance of Ambiguity Relationship

Among the Indian studies most prominent is that of Raychaudhuri (1966) who in his study Aesthetic Interest, Education Millieu Difference and Tolerance of Ambiguity examined the existence of few supposed correlates of "tolerance and acceptance of ambiguity". For this study 185 *S*s were individually given the Revised Art Scale of Welsh Figure Preference Test (RA-WFPT), the Rorschach (only the total responses with F^{+}), and Budner's Intolerance-Tolerance of Ambiguity Scale. The results showed hardly any evidence in support of the role of milieu difference in the genesis of tolerance of ambiguity. The data, of course, gave credence to the contention that tolerance and acceptance of ambiguity is positively related to artistic-aesthetic interests. In other words, the subjects recorded their preference for situations lacking in 'stimulus-boundness' and familiar cues, and containing varying degrees of apparent insolubility, openness and complexity (Frankel-Brunswik, 1949, 1951 ; Stein, 1953). It was concluded that although the tolerance of ambiguity and acceptance of perceptual complexity is related to artistic-aesthetic interest, yet they do not develop as a function of millieu difference, cultural and educational refinement and sophistication and changing historical events such as transition from agricultural social system to industrialization.

Investigating into the personality correlates of dogmatism, Hasan (1974) concluded that an individual who is tolerant of ambiguity is definitely flexible in so far as he is free from the internal compulsion to pigeon-hole the information he has been receiving from the outside world. It is due to cognitive flexibility that one who is tolerant of ambiguity, instead of hastily restructuring the situation in terms of inappropriate but readily available categories, remains in a state of suspended judgment for a relatively longer period of time. Another manifestation of cognitive flexibility on the part of a person who is tolerant of ambiguity is that he does not cling to the first impression that he has formed about a stimulus and that he is sensitive to the changes that may be imperceptibly occurring in the stimulus condition.

Goyal (1972) compared high creative and low creative groups from a sample of 300 school students with regard to their personality characteristics. It was found that high creatives have open minds, they reject repression and suppression as mechanisms for the control of impulses, and can tolerate ambiguity and entertain opposing values. Similar views were expressed by Blade (1963) when he stated : "more important for creative engineers may be their ability to perceive order from disorder, to find new solutions, to discover through methods of "cut and try", to fancy, imagine, and be ingenious".

Research Extensive but Results Inconclusive

After examining the literature available on certain intellective and non-intellective factors associated with creativity, it appears evident that research into the characteristics of the creative problem-solver is extensive but inconclusive. Engineers of near genius have been patently creative, as have engineers with moderate intelligence scores. Personality characteristics are also difficult to generalise about. But there seems to be a reasonable unanimity on the score that creative person is distinguished, most generally, by two fundamental traits, one intellective and the other motivational and attitudinal. Creativity, in other words, is not entirely a cognitive process, nor it is entirely a result of complex set of personality traits (Raina and Shukla, 1972). Another fact revealed by the review is that most of the investigations upon technical and engineering creativity have been concerned with scientists rather than engineers. Furthermore, most of the work has been carried out in the U.S. No analytical studies have been conducted to identify those needs of polytechnics which would improve the quality of instruction and ensure better outputs, growth, and development (Saran *et al.*, 1977). It is the purpose of this thesis, therefore, to systematically investigate into the factors which are associated with engineering creativity in Indian settings which may provide a base for curriculum innovations in engineering schools such that our future engineers may get out of the mental rut and be able to view problems from different vantage points and "spin off" along the tangent of risk-taking and uncertainty rather than perpetuating the circle of conformity and orthodoxy.

CHAPTER V

Methodology of the Study

Selection of Subjects

There are four diploma-level engineering institutions in the Union Territory of Delhi out of which three are meant for boys and the remaining one exclusively for girls. These institutions are run by Delhi Administration and are affiliated to the Board of Technical Education, Delhi for examination purposes. The diploma-level engineering institutions popularly known as polytechnics offer a variety of engineering courses *viz* : Mechanical Engineering, Electrical Engineering, Civil Engineering and the like with the ultimate aim of preparing technician engineers or engineering diplomates with specialization in one of the engineering branches of their choice. A preliminary survey of these institutions and their curricula revealed that Mechanical Engineering as a field of specialization is available only in boy's polytechnics. The lone Women Polytechnic does not offer courses in this branch of engineering. Hence the subjects for the present study were drawn from all the boys polytechnics of Delhi (n=522). The total population of boys studying in Mechanical Engineering branch during the session 1977-78 formed the sample. The age of the *S*s ranged from sixteen to twenty three plus years.

Determination of Groups

The Purdue Creativity Test (Lawshe and Harris, 1960) and the Culture Fair Intelligence Test (Cattell and Cattell, 1959) were administered in group situation to the original sample of 522 students (122 *S*s were dropped in the final analysis as data on all the six instruments were not available for them). The scores achieved by each subject in the two tests were instrumental in the determination of group assignment.

On the Purdue Creativity Test, scores for fluency and flexibility were obtained. Total score for the test was computed by adding the Flexibility Score to one-half the Fluency Score. The scores of fluency, flexibility and total creativity were converted into T-scores. The subjects were classified into four groups namely High Creative-High Intelligence, High Creative-Low Intelligence, Low Creative-High Intelligence and Low Creative-Low Intelligence. In arriving at these four groups the median point of distribution for the total creativity index and intelligence scores was used.

The classification system along with the sample sizes of four groups is given in Table 8 below.

TABLE 8

Sample Sizes for Four Groups, High and Low in Creativity and Intelligence

		CREATIVITY	
		High	Low
INTELLIGENCE	High	N=102	N=92
	Low	N=101	N=105

Based on the above classification four groups each for the nine independent variables *i e.* thirty-six sheets were prepared indicating scores obtained by individuals for each variable groupwise. In addition twelve more groups were formed with scores on figures of three levels of complexity in the Perceptual Simplicity-Complexity Test.

Instruments Used

A number of psychometric measures were used for the collection of the data for this study. Description of these instruments is presented below :

Purdue Creativity Test

The basic test of divergent thinking abilities in this study was the Purdue Creativity Test by C. H. Lawshe and D. H. Harris (1960). This test measures creativity in engineering. It "was developed to aid in the selection and placement of engineering personnel in positions requiring the production of a number of original ideas for the solution of problems".

Reviewing this test, Merrifield (1965) expressed the view that "this test appears to have been soundly developed, with reliability adequate for use . . . . in general, this test should be quite useful". The test is available in two forms and can be used in the "identification of design engineers who have the capacity to be really creative in the designs they produce. and research and development engineers whose success depends upon the production of new ideas".

The purpose of this test is to find out how "fluent, flexible and original" engineering personnel are in their thinking.

Scoring of the Purdue Creativity Test

The *Purdue Creativity Test*, Form H, consists of twenty items, each appearing on a separate page.

Items 1-8. Each item is a three dimensional drawing of an object together with the instructions : "List as many possible uses as you can for this object".

Items 9-12. Each item is a three dimensional drawing of two objects together with the instructions : "List as many possible uses as you can for these two objects when they are used together".

Items 13-20. Each item is a line drawing together with the question : "What is this ?" and the instructions : "List as many possibilities as you can."

Two sub scores are obtained for the test. The Flexibility Score is obtained from responses to items 1-12 and is based upon the number of different categories of uses represented by responses to each item. The Fluency Score is obtained from responses to items 13-20 and is based upon the number of different responses to each item. The total score is obtained by adding the flexibility subscore to one half the fluency subscore.

The Flexibility Score is based upon the number of different categories of uses represented by responses to each item. The list of categories together with examples of responses belonging to each category is given below :

1. *Holding—Supporting :* (bracket, chair, sling nail, coupling, reel, buckle, fence).
2. *Transfer Motion :* (roller, treadmill, crank, vibrator, pulley, gear, bearing bush, lever, cam),
3. *Regulating—Guiding :* (diffusing, template, spigot, sighting, releasing, clutch, fuse, pattern).
4. *Transfer Objects :* (fluid, funnel, piping, blotter, hoist, elevator, ramp, vehicle, stairs, doors).
5. *Shielding Protecting :* (headwear, bumperguard, covering, sealing, muzzle, shelter).
6. *Forming Tool :* (cutting, punching, drill, rake, die, compressing, plow, comb).
7. *Measuring and Marketing :* (gauge, target, testing, counting, scales, thermometer).
8. *Supply Power :* (motor spring, power source).
9. *Making Sound :* (musical instrument, tuning fork, making noise).
10. *Communicating :* (pointing, sign, indexing, indicator, letter of the alphabet, signalling).

11. *Heating* : (transfer heat, heat exchanger).
12. *Trapping Animal* : (mouse trap, etc.).
13. *Instructional Objects* : (cone, cylinder, pyramid, sphere, eraser).
14. *Decorating Objects* : (flower pot, vase, etc.).
15. *Magnetic Objects* : (magnet, magnetic core).
16. *Ornamental Objects* : (bangles, rings).
17. *Household Items* : (jar, drum, tray, glass, dust-bin, box, bucket, basket, vessel, container).
18. *Lighting* : (picture tube, photography-light, shade-light, head-light, fancy-light).
19. *Striking Objects* : (bullet, gun, weapon, arrow, hammer).
20. *Fastening Devices* : (locking device, lock nut, jib and cotter, wedge).
21. *Raw Materials* : (raw materials in work-shop, job in shops, object in machine).
22. *Sports Objects* : (Javelene, Wickets, Seesaw, Exercise bars, C.G. toys).
23. *Fixing Devices* : (Jaws, chucks, vice, clamp).

While scoring, any such responses that are of a general nature are eliminated from consideration. The number of different categories listed for each item are then counted allowing one point for each different category. The sum of the points is the flexibility score for that item. An addition of all these scores for items 1-12 gives the Flexibility Score for the test.

Reliability

Two kinds of reliability estimates are given for the flexibility score : an interscorer correlation of .87 and a split half reliability coefficient of .86. Split-half reliabilities of .93 and .95 are reported for the fluency and total scores, respectively. The interscorer correlation for total score was .91.

Validity

Concurrent Validity of the creativity scores investigated in three groups of professional engineers demonstrate that the test is quite valid. The generalized validity for Total Score was also investigated for all 104 product (N=33), process (N=29) and project (N=42) engineers. Norms based on total scores for 106 professional engineers working in industry are provided in the manual.

Flexibility, Fluency, and Total Scores were correlated with the Wonderlic Personnel Test—a test of mental alertness, and the Mechanical Comprehension Test Form CC. Their product-moment correlations are presented in Table 9. The correlations indicated that the Creativity Scores were not measuring the same abilities as these other two tests.

TABLE 9

Correlations between Creativity Scores and other Tests

	Wonderlic *N=48*	*Mech. Comp. (CC)* *N=43*
Fluency	.15	—.08
Flexibility	.15	.13
Total Score	.16	—.01

Reliability and Validity in India

It is evident from the foregoing description that reliability and validity for the test have satisfactorily been established by the authors. Nevertheless it was thought proper to establish them in our own cultural context. Although it could be used with fair amount of confidence otherwise also as the test is entirely figural.

In order to establish reliability and validity of the test in Indian settings following procedure was adopted :

Two kinds of reliability estimates namely the test-retest reliability and an inter-scorer reliability were established for the test in question.

Test-Retest Reliability

With a view to establish the test-retest reliability a sample of 60 students studying in first and second year of Electrical Engineering branch were tested and retested with an interval of about six months in between. As the sections of these students in the institution were made on random basis these were considered as random groups. The test-retest coefficient of correlation computed from the data thus obtained came out to be .74 (significant at .01 level).

Interscorer Reliability

In order to establish the interscorer reliability for the present test a sample of 20 test-booklets were got re-scored by another scorer (a mechanical engineer) independently. An interscorer correlation cofficient was then calculated which worked out of be .98 (significant at .01 level) for Flexibility scores ; .99 (significant at .01 level) for Fluency scores and .98 (significant at .01 level) for Total-Creativity scores.

Validity

The suggestion put forth by Yamamoto (1965, 1967) that "In studies of creative thinking, ratings by informed teachers who have been given enough time to get acquainted with their children would seem to be able to distinguish the creative pupils from the less creative ones when asked to nominate them on specific criteria . . ." seems to be quite pertinent and worthwhile. Hence on similar lines the investigator in this study personally contacted the staff members of mechanical Engineering and distributed the check lists on 'Teacher Evaluation on Creativity' (Torrance, 1966) to them. Particular care was taken to include only those lecturers for ranking the students, as most fluent and least fluent ; most flexible and least flexible, who had direct and continuous contact with the students and their projects. A total of 25 check lists were analysed for establishing the validity of the Purdue Creativity Test used in this study. The *t* test was applied to each of the mean test scores of the most fluent and least fluent subjects and the most flexible and least flexible subjects. This test was used to determine whether or not a significant difference existed between the two means. The value of *t* came out to be 3.62 (significant at .01 level of significance) between the means of most fluent and least fluent and 1.92 (significant at .10 level of significance) between the means of most flexible and least flexible.

It is on the basis of the above findings that the test has been used with confidence in this study.

Culture Fair Intelligence Test

Culture Fair Intelligence Test, Scale 3 designed by Cattell and Cattell (1959) has been used in this study. Scale 3 operates at over 14 years and through the superior adult level, being especially suitable for spreading out finely the ability differences of university undergraduate and graduate students. According to the manual, in the use of scale 3 for educational guidance between undergraduate and graduate colleges a truer comparison among candidates in arts, science, engineering etc. can be made than with analogies, synonyms etc. and tests couched wholly in verbal, literary terms. Both from the stand-point of pure research, where a clear concept of intelligence is to be related to other variables, and of applied psychology, where practical efficiency is important, the rooting of the C.F. tests in basic theoretical research is a great advantage. In the first place, the meaning of validity, and the possibility of assessing it objectively under various circumstances, are provided by the fact of these scales' having emerged from Spearman's theory of general ability, and Thurstone's second order factor among the established primary abilities. By this touchstone, the C.F. tests can be shown to be among the few most highly valid intelligence tests in existence.

The test under discussion consists of four sub-tests. Items and time alloted to each subtest in Scale 3 are given in Table 10.

TABLE 10

Items and Time Allotted to Each Subtest in Scale 3

	Number of Items	*Time Allotted*
Test 1 Series	13	3 mins.
Test 2 Classifications	14	4 mins.
Test 3 Matrices	13	3 mins.
Test 4 Conditions (Topology)	10	2 1/2 mins.
Total	50 items	12 1/2 mins.

Although the actual testing time as mentioned above is 12 1/2 minutes, but with time taken by instructions, filling out the cover page etc. makes it about 25 to 30 minutes. In the arrangement of subtests, a comparatively well known, easy to-grasp test has been chosen to start the subject off. In all tests the component items are arranged to occur in order of increasing difficulty. All the four subtests-Series, Classifications, Matrices and Topology—have about equal intercorrelation and substantial "g" saturation. The instructions to be given during administration are set out in *verbatim* form.

Scoring of the answer sheets was done by a stencil key fitted exactly over the sheet, and giving one point for each item right. If more than one answer was marked for an item in tests 1, 3, or 4 no credit was given for that item. An addition of the number of answers correct for each of the four subtests gives the "Total Raw Score."

Reliability

Test reliability, the authors state, has been evaluated both in terms of the Dependability Coefficient and the Homogeneity Coefficient. The Dependability Coefficient (agreement on test-retest without time lapse) has extended from .84 to .94 on four undergraduate groups of slightly more than 100 each. With long time interval, so that it becomes a Stability Coefficient, in which real function fluctuation of the ability itself is involved, it may be 15 points lower and in Rodd's Taiwan data (1958) fell as low as .53. Knapp's experiment separated "power" from "speed" administration and found reliabilities ranging from .71 to .92 on the former and .71 to .94 on the latter.

The Homogeneity Coefficient (as a split-half, corrected to full length) came out on three recent undergrauate groups (100, 155, and 212) at .82, .91 and .95.

By the nature of the test, correlations with *past* achievement should be lower than for achievement-contaminated traditional intelligence tests. This proves to be the case, the mean *r* with general achievement running so far at .61 (N=53, 191 and 155). This provides a clearer statement of how much of achievement is due to ability rather than recent opportunity and permits a more accurate prediction for the individual case when ability and achievement components are separately assessed.

Validity

The primary evidence of the validity of an intelligence test is its direct correlation with the general ability factor as determined uniquely by factor analyses, According to the original published researches (Cattell *et. al.* 1941) and others since (Buros, 1959 ; Geist, 1954 ; Marquent and Bailey, 1955 ; Pierce-Jones and Tylor, 1950 ; Tilton, 1949) the correlations with "g" of the four types of sub-test range through .53, .68, 89 and .99 (the last obviously raised and the first probably dropped by sampling error). A recent study on the edition used in France, by the Centre de Psychologie Applique'e, on a very ample sample found all 'g' correlations of these Culture-Free subtests to range between .78 and .83, while Bajard (1955) found saturations ranging in different samples from .71 to .84, all of which demonstrate a very gratifying level for tests of such brevity.

According to reviews in Buros Mental Measurements Yearbook (1959, 1953) the C.F. shows an *r* with the Revised Stanford Binet of .56 (later studies have yielded .71), with the Otis of .73, and with the A.C.E. of .59. Recent studies by Bensberg and Sloan (1955) show a correlation with the Stanford Binet of .85, while Tilton (1949) finds a correlation of .84 with the Wechsler Bellevue.

The test because of its well established reliability and validity has been extensively used by researchers both in our country and outside.

Mechanical Reasoning Test

This test forms a part of Differential Aptitude Test Battery. It consists of pictorially presented items of mechanical situations together with simply worded questions on each individual item. Care was taken to present items in terms of simple, frequently encountered mechanisms that do not resemble text book illustrations or require special knowledge.

There is reason for considerable confidence in the Mechanical Reasoning Test. It was built with the full experience of the Bennet Mechanical Comprehension Tests behind it. The extensive literature reported in recent years has amply demonstrated the usefulness of this approach to reasoning in the mechanical field and the success with which the test measures understanding of mechanical and physical principles in familiar situations. The Mechanical Reasoning Test was devised to parallel closely Form AA of the regular series of Mechanical Comprehension Tests, with some minor changes suggested by experience with the earlier tests and with forms devised by Bennett for military classification use.

The ability measured by the Mechanical Reasoning Test may be regarded as one aspect of intelligence, if intelligence is broadly defined. The person who stands high in this characteristic finds it easy to learn the principles of operation and repair of complex devices. The score is affected by the previous experience of the subject but not to a degree that introduces serious difficulties in interpretation. Formal training in Physics produces an increase in score of only a few points.

The test is useful in those curricula and occupations where an appreciation of the principles of common physical forces is required. If a student intending to major in a physical science field, or in technical or manual training courses, does not make a good score on this test, he should expect to find the work difficult. Occupations such as those of carpenter, mechanic, maintenance-man, assembler, and hundreds of others in plants and factories require the kind of understanding it measures.

It is important to note that Mechanical Reasoning scores are of less educational and vocational significance for girls than for boys. The mean scores for girls are lower, the reliability of measurement is poorer, and the value of the test for educational and vocational guidance is less clearly established for females. If a girl expresses interest in mechanical or engineering work her score probably will be more meaningful if compared with the scores of boys in her grade rather than with those of girls.

The test consists of 68 questions to be answered in 30 minutes. For scoring the test there is a Rights key and a Wrongs key. The score for a subject is the number of Right answers minus one-half the number of Wrong answers (R—1/2 W). Norms for the test expressed in terms of rank equivalents are available in the manual.

Study of Values

Several investigators of creative personality have used the Allport-Vernon-Lindzey Study of Values (1960) designed to measure in the individual the relative strengths of the six values of men as described by Spranger, the German psychologist and educator—the theoretical, the economic, the aesthetic, the social, the political, and the religious. The value test as used in the present study has been prepared in Hindi by R.K. Ojha and is identical to Allport-Vernon-Lindzey Scale of Values.

The test consists of a total of 45 questions divided into two parts. The first part includes 30 questions and each question is provided with two alternatives as possible answers. There are 15 questions in part two and each question has four alternatives as possible answers. In this way there are in all 120 answers divided equally among the six values. The subject while replying to the questions has to write those numbers in a particular order for which directions are given in the test itself. These numbers are then added for each value resulting in raw scores which are entered in the scoring table.

At the formative stages of the present scale a large spectrum of student community drawn from diverse areas of speciality including that of Engineering group formed the sample of the study. This Indian adaption of AVL has been used by many researchers in India since its inception.

Reliability

The reliability of this test was found by employing the Split-half technique and the Kudar Richardson technique by the author. The reliability data thus obtained are presented below :

TABLE 11

Split-half Reliability

Sample	*Theoretical*	*Economic*	*Aesthetic*	*Social*	*Political*	*Religious*
I	.64	.51	.58	.72	.76	.56
II & III	.70	.59	.51	.69	.78	.79
IV	.48	.69	.80	.59	.41	.88
V	.45	.78	.48	.60	.50	.90
VI	.55	.71	.49	.72	.79	.61
VII	.66	.61	.40	.59	.49	.62
VIII	.71	.67	.79	.68	.51	.59
Total Group	.60	.65	.58	.66	.61	.71

TABLE 12

Reliability of Kudar Rechardson

Theoretical	*Economic*	*Aesthetic*	*Social*	*Political*	*Religious*
.70	.80	.69	.89	.88	.71

Validity

Regarding the validity of the test the author states that

since standardised value-tests were not available in Hindi, the validity of the present value-test was established by computing Product-moment correlations amongst different values. The correlation coefficients obtained are shown in Table 13 below :

TABLE 13

Values	*Economic*	*Aesthetic*	*Social*	*Political*	*Religious*
Theoretical	+.32	—.40	—.39	—.62	+.32
Economic		+.48	+.46	+.56	+.60
Aesthetic			—.38	—.49	—.50
Social				+.57	—.54
Political					—.34

The auther has taken these coefficients of correlation as an index of the validity of the test.

For a proper understanding of the real import of each value, their respective definitions, as given in 'Study of Values' (Allport, *et. al.* 1960) are presented below :

a. Theoretical

The theoretical value reflects a dominant interest in the discovery of truth. In achieving this goal, one takes a "cognitive" attitude which enables him to look for identities and differences ; he also divests himself of judgments regarding the beauty or utility of objects, and seeks only to observe and reason. The thoeretical value-orientation reflects empirical, critical, rational and intellectualistic tendency on the part of the individual.

b. Economic

The economic man is characteristically interested in what is useful. Based originally upon the satisfaction of bodily needs (self preservation), the interest in utilities develops to embrace the practical affairs of the business world—the production, marketing and consumption of goods, the elaboration of credit and the accumulation of tangible wealth. This type is thoroughly practical.

c. **Aesthetic**

The aesthetic value is characterized by form and harmony. Each single experience is judged from the standpoint of grace, symmetry, or fitness under this condition. This value-orientation regards life as a procession of events where each single impression is enjoyed for its own sake. The chief interest that characterizes this value-orientation is the aesthetic approach which need not be oriented in achievement.

d. **Social**

The highest value for this type is love of people. In the 'Study of Values', it is the altruistic or philanthropic aspect of love that is measured. The social man prizes other persons as ends, and is, therefore, himself kind, sympathetic and unselfish. He is likely to find the theoretical, economic and aesthetic attitudes cold and inhuman. In contrast to the political type, the social man regards love as itself the only suitable form of human relationship. (Spranger adds that in its purest form the social interest is selfless and tends to approach very closely to the religious attitude).

e. **Political**

The political man is interested primarily in power. His activities are not necessarily within the narrow field of politics. Leaders in any field generally have high power value. Since competition and struggle play a large part in all life, many philosophers have seen power as the most universal and most fundamental of motives. There are, however, certain personalities in whom the desire for a direct expression of this motive is uppermost, who wish, above all else, for personal power, influence and renown.

f. **Religious**

The highest value of the religious man may be called unity.

He is mystical and seeks to comprehend the cosmos as a whole, to relate himself to its embracing totality (Spranger defines the religious man as one whose mental structure is permanently directed to the creation of the highest and abolutely satisfying value experience). He with his zest and enthusiasm sees something divine in every event. In many individuals "the negation and affirmation of life alternate to yield the greatest satisfaction".

Perceptual Simplicity-Complexity Test

In most of the recent studies with regard to the preferences for simplicity and complexity of polygons, painting or even poems, many important characteristics of the persons were recognised. Aesthetic preferences of a person were associated with certain characteristics of that person (Knapp & Wulf, Johnson & Knapp, Duprez, Hammes, Husnipalacios & Palacios). Simple Vs. Complex paintings and polygons were associated with certain personality differences and it was found that complex polygons were preferred by creative arts students and comparably simple forms of polygons were preferred by less creative students. Thus most frequently simplicity or complexity was assessed on the basis of simple or complex polygons. Simplicity of Complexity of ploygon was defined by the number of points in that polygon.

Since many important conclusions about an individual's personality have been drawn with the preferences of simple or complex polygons an instrument namely Perceptual Simpicity-Complexity Test of geometrical figures was designed by Chawla (1970) using semantic differential technique. It is this instrument which has been used in the present study for finding out the perceptual preferences of creative engineers.

The test consists of 15 geometrical figures which have been designated as most simple, intermediate and most complex by the author. Each level of complexity includes five figures. The author of the test prescribes ranking of each figure by the subjects on eight bipolar adjectives on a 7 point semantic differential scale. The scale is presented in Vable 14.

TABLE 14

Form of Simplicity—Complexity Scale

Clear	———————————————	Hazy
Concentrate	———————————————	Diffuse
Definite	———————————————	Uncertain
Even	———————————————	Uneven
Simple	———————————————	Complex
Usual	———————————————	Unusual
Vague	———————————————	Precise
Obvious	———————————————	Subtle

Before using the test for the present study following procedure was adopted :

a. All the fifteen figures were randomized such that the figures, in the form of a booklet, are presented to the subjects in this randomized sequence.

b. The eight bipolar adjectives were randomized.

c. The ends of these bipolar adjectives were also randomized.

The final set of adjectives which emerged after the aforesaid randomization procedure is given below which accompanies every figure in the booklet.

Obvious	.... : .... : .... : .... :	Subtle
Concentrate	.... : .... : .... : .... :	Diffuse
Unusual	.... : .... : .... : .... :	Usual
Simple	.... : .... : .... : .... :	Complex
Uneven	.... : .... : .... : .... :	Even
Vague	.... : .... : .... : .... :	Precise
Uncertain	.... : .... : .... : .... :	Definite
Hazy	.... : .... : .... : .... :	Clear

As shown above each bi-polar adjective has seven spaces in between. The subject is required to judge each figure, as printed on the top of each page, by placing a tick mark in one of the seven spaces on each line. These spaces represent in say Hazy-Clear continuum as very Hazy, Quite Hazy, Slightly Hazy, Equally Hazy or Clear, Slightly Clear, Quite Clear and Very Clear. The closer the tick-mark put by the subject to one or the other of the opposites on a line the closer he judges the figure to be related to that adjective. The complete procedure of judging each figure has been illustrated by an example in the opening pages of the booklet. If a tick-mark is put in the fourth or the middle space it would mean judging the figure to be equally related to both of the adjectives. The subjects were warned : "Never put more than one tick mark on any one line and do not omit any of the lines".

Scoring for each adjective is done in positive direction only according to the space ticked by the subject. A mean for each figure is then calculated from the obtained scores.

The means thus obtainted were tabulated under 'most simple', 'intermediate' and 'most complex' figures for every subject. Along with this the mean of all the fifteen means for each subject too was computed giving one mean score for each individual on the test. Separate analyses were done for the data thus obtained by pursuing the two ways of consolidating the scores.

Reliability

A test-retest reliability coefficient of .87 (significant at .01 level of significance) has been reported by the author of the test on a sample of 32 subjects.

Validity

It has been stated by the author that the test has got face validity.

Reliability for the Present Study

In addition a test-retest reliability was established by the investigator himself for the present study as well. For this purpose a sample of 60 students studying in first and second year of electrical engineering branch were tested and re-tested with an interval of about six months in between. The test-retest coefficient of correlation computed from the data thus obtained came out to be .71 (significant at .01 level of significance).

The Budner Tolerance-Intolerance of Ambiguity Scale

According to Budner (1962), intolerance of ambiguity means "the tendency to perceive i. e., interpret ambiguous situations as sources of threat". An ambiguous situation is defined as one which cannot be adequately structured or categorised by the individual. Budner mentions three such situations : (i) the completely new situation in which there are no familiar cues ; (ii) a complex situation in which there are a great number of cues to be taken into account ; (iii) a contradictory situation in which different elements or cues suggest different structures. In short, situations characterised by novelty, complexity or insolubility present instances of ambiguous situations. Individuals respond to stimuli on at least two levels : (i) the phenomenological and (ii) the operative. The question is : what reactions at these two levels suggest perception of threat ? According to Budner, the range of possible reactions to threat may be dichotomised crudely into submission and denial. By submission, he meant the recognition of the situation as an ineluctable fact of existence which the individual cannot alter. By denial, he meant the performance of some act by which the objective reality, even if only in the phenomenological world of the individual, is altered to suit the desires of the perceiver. Budner (1962) writes : "Thus, if an individual exhibits any one of the following types of response phenomenological denial (repression and denial), phenomenological submission (anxiety and discomfort), operative denial (destructive or reconstructive behaviour), or operative submission (avoidance behaviour)-it seems plausible to infer that he is, in some way, threatened. If these behaviours are elicited by situations characterized by novelty, complexity, or insolubility, it would seem reasonable to infer that the individual is intolerant of ambiguity." (p. 30).

Keeping in view the above meaning of intolerance of ambiguity, Budner (1962) developed the scale of Tolerance-Intolerance of Ambiguity. This scale consists of 16 items, of which 8 are positively and 8 negatively worded. Six response categories : Strongly, moderately or slightly agree and strongly, moderately, or slightly disagree are written against each item. On positively worded items, Strong agreement is scored 7, moderate agreement 6, slight agreement 5, slight disagreement 3, moderate disagreement 2, and strong ditagreement 1. Scoring of negative items was in the reverse direction. For each item omitted, a score of 4 is given. The higher the score of a subject, the greater is his intolerance of ambiguity. The reliabilities were computed by means of Cronbach's Alpha Formula (Guilford 1954) by using the data of 13 samples. The range of reliability coefficients was from .39 to .62, the mean being approximately .49. One sample was administered this scale twice. For this group, a test-retest correlation of .85 was obtained. Validation data included correlations with other scales of intolerance of ambiguity, with ranking of individuals on the basis of short autobiographies, and with Peer's ratings. The correlation between this scale and the Coulter scale as reported by Eysenck (1954) was found to be .36. Similarly, its correlations with Princeton Scale (Sounders, 1955) and Walk Scale (O' Connor 1952) were obtained as .50 and .54 respectively. This scale has been used by Shanker (1970) in his Ph. D. thesis.

Statistical Analyses

To test the hypotheses of the present study following statistical techniques were used :—

a. Creativity Intelligence Groups

The scores obtained for fluency, flexibility and total creativity were first transformed into T scores for each subject. The subjects were then classified into four groups, based on their joint standing on creativity index and intelligence score, *viz* : the High-Creative High Intelligence, the High Creative-Low Intelligence, the Low Creative-High Intelligence and the Low Creative-Low Intelligence. In arriving at these four groups, the median points of distribution for total-creativity index and intelligence scores were used.

b. 2x2 Analysis of Variance

For the four-fold classification of the subjects described above, 2x2 analyses of variance technique was adopted. For unequal number in the subclasses proper treatment was given to arrive at an exact solution.

c. Comparison of Means

d. Correlational Analysis

e. Intercorrelations

f. Stepwise Multiple Regression Analysis

g. Factor Analysis.

CHAPTER VI

The Characteristics of Creative Engineers

As stated earlier, the final sample for the study consisted of 400 *S*s for whom complete data on all the variables were available. These subjects were almost exclusively from middle-class socio-economic status families whose fathers had monthly income ranging from Rs. 201 to Rs. 1000 and had the following occupational roles : middle class administrators, government servants, teachers, big shopkeepers, engineers and the like. They had the same educational level and belonged to the same sex (male) ; the mean age of the sample was 18 years 5 months as calculated to the nearest month of the testing time.

The total sample was then distributed among the four subgroups as described in the previous chapter. These four subgroups were subsequently compared on all the ten variables by a series of 2×2 analyses of variance. For this comparison of the four subgroups of subjects the scores on mechanical reasoning ; theoretical, economical, aesthetic, social, political and religious values ; simplicity-complexity – (combined ; on 'most sample' figures ; on 'intermediate' figures and on 'most complex' figures) and intolerance of ambiguity have been treated individually and their results alongwith discussions is presented in the following pages.

Mechanical Reasoning—an aid to engineering creativity

The results point out (Table 15) that the mean scores on mechanical reasoning of the high (29.44) and the low (26.58) creativity groups are not significantly different at the 0.1 level of significance but the difference becomes significant at .05 level of significance. This shows a positive effect of creativity on mechanical reasoning.

The results of the study, therefore, indicate that the high-creative individuals perform significantly higher on the Mechanical Reasoning Ability Test than their low-creative counterparts.

This probably indicates that an understanding and appreciation of the principles of common mechanical and physical forces is helpful towards creativity in mechanical engineering field. It is in conformity with the Views of Owens (1974) who stated : "Mechanical Comprehension should be an integral part of engineering creativity". However, there is a general lack of researches in this area.

TABLE 15

Mean Scores of Mechanical Reasoning for the Four Groups

N=400

		CREATIVITY High	CREATIVITY Low
INTELLIGENCE	High	32.38 (11.64)	30.64 (10.85)
	Low	26.47 (10.85)	23.03 (10.00)
	Total	29.44 (11.63)	26.58 (11.08)

ANALYSIS OF VARIANCE

Source	df	MS	*F*	*p*
Creativity	1	6.702921	5.64	*
Intelligence	1	45.765225	38.516	**
Interaction	1	0.719104	0.6052	n.s.
Error	396	1.1882		

Note : In this and all subsequent ?x2 Tables, standard deviations appe^r in parentheses and
* .05 level of significance
** .01 level of significance

Further a highly significant effect is seen in the case of Intelligence but interaction effect is insignificant. This is hardly surprising in view of the fact that mechanical reasoning has been regarded as one aspect of intelligence, if intelligence is broadly defined.

The findings of the present study when viewed in the perspective of a professional group in the specific field of mechanical engineering indicate that to be creative in such fields and to arrive at unusual but socially useful, economically feasible and hitherto unknown configurations a basic mechanical aptitude and specific reasoning ability towards familiar mechanical and physical situations is an aid to creativity. In this context, intelligence is best taken to mean competence in the skills and knowledge relevant to the area of work, a view implicit in Kuhn's (1963) suggestion that you have to be a traditionalist before you can be an innovator. Somewhat similar conclusions were arrived at by Buhl (1958) who, studying freshman engineers as subjects, found a close correlation between creativity and scholastic achievement at the end of the college freshman year.

High Economical Value—an important personality characteristic

In the present section, it will be inquired whether the four sub-groups of subjects delineated previously distinguish on the six values namely Theoretical, Economical, Aesthetic, Social, Political and Religious as defined by the scales of values (Allport-Vernon-Lindzey, 1960). For this purpose each value will be taken at a time and the mean and standard deviation for each will be presented within the four sub-groups generated by the intelligence and creativity dimensions. By analysis of variance procedure it will be examined whether the variations in the mean are a systematic function of intelligence, creativity or combination of the two (interaction).

(a) Theoretical Value

The theoretical value reflects a dominant interest in the discovery of truth. In achieving this goal, one takes a "cognitive" attitude which enables him to look for identities and differences ; he also divests himself of judgments regarding the beauty or utility of objects, and seeks only to observe and reason. The theoretical value-orientation reflects empirical, critical, rational and intellectualistic tendency on the part of the individual.

The results, as shown in Table 16, explicitly point out that the mean scores on theoretical value of the high (45.49) and the low (45.51) creativity group are not significantly different from one another. No significant effect is seen in the case of intelligence either, and interaction effect is also insignificant. The groups are, therefore, homogeneous as far as theoretical value is concerned. The proposed hypothesis, therefore, stands confirmed and the present results seem to be a departure from the findings of the previous researches (MacKinnon, 1963 ; Heist, 1968 ; Eiduson, 1957, 1958, 1962 ; Yamamoto, 1963 ; Drevedahl, 1964 and Paramesh, 1970).

The findings of the present study may be viewed in the light of the present professional group which happens to be mechanical engineers. The studies contending that high theo-

TABLE 16

Mean Scores of Theoretical Value for Four Groups

N=400

		CREATIVITY	
		High	Low
INTELLIGENCE	High	45.96 (6.75)	45.21 (6.97)
	Low	45.02 (5.94)	45.77 (6.63)
	Total	45.49 (6.40)	45.51 (6.78)

ANALYSIS OF VARIANCE

Source	df	MS	*F*	*p*
Creativity	1	.00000169	.0000038	n.s.
Intelligence	1	·035344	.0808	n.s.
Interaction	1	.56685841	1.29	n.s.
Error	396	.437212		

retical value characterise creative individuals; have studied architects, artists, teachers or school students. No evidence is available regarding technician engineer whose prime concern is not simply to seek truth for its own sake or just to observe and to reason divesting himself of judgments regarding the beauty or utility of objects, but is more interested in what is useful and productive. The practice of engineering is by and large hedged with limitations. In solving engineering problems these limits are generally very restrictive and involve public or governmental policies ; the limits of cost, specific materials, time, known scientific principles which can be utilised, size, shape, manpower, appearance, auxiliary services available; and restrictive codes, methods and procedures, union labour rules and other limits. As a result, the most important feature of engineering problem-solving and design is compromise. It is rare that the final solution is the "best" one.

(b) Economical Value

Economical Value is characterized by what is useful and thoroughly practical. Great feats of engineering and application result from the demand economic men make upon science. The economic men regard unapplied knowledge as waste. Results indicate, as presented in Table 17, significant effect in the case of creativity on economical value. The effects of intelligence and creativity-intelligence interaction remain insignificant. The mean for high-creativity group is 44.80, while for the low-creativity group it is 43.33. 'This shows a positive effect of creativity on economical value'. The hypothesis that high-creative individuals are not significantly different from their low-creative counterparts on economical value is, therefore, rejected. While the result is in conformity with Blatt and Stein (1957), it does not agree with MacKinnon (1963) and Welberg and Welsh (1967) who found innovatives to be lower on economical value.

Historically and characteristically, science has used the adjective "theoretical" to describe its activities, while engineering has insisted upon the adjective "practical" (Walker, 1963). In conformity with the economic attitude which is characterised by utility and the application of knowledge for practical but economic propositions a creative engineer too recognizes that knowledge, in and of itself is sterile and useless. It becomes important only after it has been put to use in the affairs of man. This is the job for which engineers are specifically trained. In this context it is quite natural that the creative engineers should be higher on economical value as revealed in the present study. It implies that a creative solution to an engineering problem, to be acceptable, has to be practical and at the same time feasible

TABLE 17

Mean Scores of Economical Value for the Four Groups

(N=400)

		CREATIVITY	
		High	Low
INTELLIGENCE	High	44.627 (6.22)	43.478 (7.87)
	Low	45.980 (7.41)	43.200 (7.75)
	Total	44.80 (6.87)	43.30 (7.81)

ANALYSIS OF VARIANCE

Source	df	MS	*F*	*p*
Creativity	1	2.144760	3.946	*
Intelligence	1	.001406	.00258	n.s.
Interaction	1	.099541	.183	n.s.
Error	396	.5434772		

within the economic constraints of man, money and material. Thus one can maintain that higher creativity in the context of a developing economy lies in the creation of such configurations which are not only novel but economically viable also such that the products remain within the reach of majority of the customers and not simply remain redundant in show rooms or godowns.

(c) Aesthetic Value

The aesthetic value is characterised by form and harmony. Each single experience is judged from the standpoint of grace, symmetry, or fitness under this condition. This value orientation regards life as a procession of events where each single impression is enjoyed for its own sake. The chief interest that characterizes this value orientation is the aesthetic approach which need not be oriented in achievement.

The results, presented in Table 18, point out that the mean scores on aesthetic value of the high (31.665) and the low (11.700) creativity groups are not significantly different from one another, although there is a slight tendency in favour of a positive effect of creativity on aesthetic value. Further, no significant effect is seen in the case of intelligence, and interaction effect is insignificant. The groups, therefore, are almost homogeneous as far as aesthetic value is concerned. However, the mean of high creatives is slightly higher than that of the low creatives. The proposed hypothesis is therefore, confirmed and the present results are a slight departure from the findings of the previous researchers (MacKinnon, 1963 ; Heist, 1968; Eiduson, 1957, 1958, 1962 ; Yamamoto, 1963; Drevdahl, 1964 and Paramesh, 1970).

The findings of the present study indicate that creative engineers in the context of a poor country and developing economy perhaps feel more concerned with import substitution, mass production of utility items at cheaper rates and economically feasible improvisations rather than perfection, beauty and aesthetic considerations. They are more concerned with the production of items which are within the purchasing capacity of common man. Luxury of aesthetic beauty in its variety and grace enters largely in the domain of affluent economy. In our country even architects are required to design buildings which are functionally oriented and can be built with modest investment. Therefore, in our cultural and economic context the result of the present study seems to be quite in tune with the demands of the society made on prospective engineers which is based more on utility and satisfaction of minimum necessities of human needs.

TABLE 18

Mean Scores of Aesthetic Value for the Four Groups
(N=400)

		CREATIVITY	
		High	Low
INTELLIGENCE	High	31.754 (7.92)	31.130 (8.23)
	Low	31.574 (8.31)	30.323 (7.32)
	Total	31.665 (3.11)	30.700 (7.76)

ANALYSIS OF VARIANCE

Source	df	MS	*F*	*p*
Creativity	1	.878906	1.379	n.s.
Intelligence	1	.243542	.382	n.s.
Interaction	1	.098233	.154	n.s.
Error	396	.6369469		

(d) Social Value

Social value is characterised by love of people. The social man prizes other persons as ends, and is, therefore, himself kind, sympathetic and unselfish. Love is regarded by him as itself the only suitable form of human relationship. Spranger adds that in its purest form the social interest is selfless and tends to approach very closely to the religious attitude.

TABLE 19

Mean Scores of Social Value for the Four Groups

(N=400)

		CREATIVITY	
		High	Low
INTELLIGENCE	High	43.392 (6.47)	42.010 (7.23)
	Low	42.910 (6.98)	43.780 (6.64)
	Total	43.153 (6.69)	42.954 (6.98)

ANALYSIS OF VARIANCE

Source	df	MS	*F*	*p*
Creativity	1	.065536	.139	n.s.
Intelligence	1	.414736	.882	n s.
Interac'ion	1	1.267876	2.297	n.s.
Error	396	.4699871		

Information concerning this dimension is provided in Table 19. The results show no significant effect for both creativity and intelligence. Interaction effect is also insignificant.

The mean scores on social value of the high (43.153) and the low (42.954) creativity groups indicate no insignificant differance from one another. The groups are, therefore, homogeneous as far as social value is concerned. The proposed hypothsis is, therefore, established. This is in conformity with the findings of Paramesh (1970) who also found no difference between high and low creative groups on social value. It, however, does not agree with that of Windholz (1968).

(e) Political Value

The prime concern of political value is power. Competition and struggle play a large part and power is seen as the most universal and most fundamental of motives. The results, as reported in Table 20, explicitly point out that the mean scores on political value of the high-creative group (38.473) and the low-creative group (38.883) are not significantly different

TABLE 20

Mean Scores of Political Value for the Four Groups
(N=400)

		CREATIVITY	
		High	Low
INTELLIGENCE	High	38.088 (5.45)	38.250 (7.59)
	Low	38.861 (5.37)	39.438 (5.71)
	Total	38.473 (5.41)	38.883 (6.68)

ANALYSIS OF VARIANCE

Source	df	MS	*F*	*p*
Creativity	1	.136530	.368	n.s.
Intelligence	1	.961380	2.595	n.s.
Interaction	1	.043057	.116	n.s.
Error	396	.3703376		

from one another. Again, no significant effect is seen in the case of intelligence, and interaction effect is insignificant. The groups are, therefore, homogeneous as far as political value is concerned. The proposed hypothesis thus stands confirmed. Results obtained in the present study support the findings of Paramesh (1970) who also found no difference on political value among the criterion groups.

TABLE 21

Mean Scores of Religious Value for the Four Groups
(N=400)

		CREATIVITY	
		High	Low
INTELLIGENCE	High	31.254 (7.25)	30 239 (8.07)
	Low	32.900 (7.37)	31.323 (9.93)
	Total	32.073 (7.35)	30 817 (7.54)

ANALYSIS OF VARIANCE

Source	df	MS	F	p
Creativity	1	1.679616	3.041	n.s.
Intelligence	1	1.863225	3.374	n s.
Interaction	1	.078961	.143	n s.
Error	396	.552276		

f. Religious value

Religious and spiritual values play a dominant role in the lives of people. They provide spiritual power and strength to cope with complex problems of life. Religion also provides a particular mode of living and conduct, and is a source of law, morality, art, music, literature and the general values of the individual. Prayer assemblage at religious places, study of religious material and listening to scripts compiled by religious gurus satisfy many needs of the individual, such as aesthetic, psychological, intellectual and metaphysical, and promote social interaction and cooperation.

It is found from the results of the present study given in Table 21 that the mean scores on religious value of the high (32.073) and the low (30.817) creativity groups are although not significantly different from one another but there is a tendency in favour of a positive effect of creativity on religious value. Further, no significant effect is seen in the case of intelligence, and interaction effect too is insignificant. The proposed hypothesis is confirmed and the present results are a departure from the findings of MacKinnon (1963), Heist (1968), Blatt and Stein (1957). While the present results are in conformity with Paramesh (1970) the higher mean in favour of the high creatives also somewhat support the contention of Pepinsky (1960) who found that the productive non-conformists were having a well-integrated set of values, whether religious, ethical, or social.

Creative Engineers Perceive Order in Disorder

Stylistic ways of using mind and style or modes of experiencing also determine to a large extent the creativity of an individual. Research in this area of perceptual complexity has consistently shown that individuals identified as highly creative seem to be able to discern and to prefer complexity in whatever it is that they attend to.

In order to test such a hypothesis scores on Perceptual Simplicity-Complexity Test used in this study was administered to the subjects. This test as explained earlier includes in all fifteen figures classified by the author in three distinct categories as follows :

Figures 5, 6, 9, 11 and 13	Most Simple
Figures 3, 4, 7, 12 and 14	Intermediate
Figures 1, 2, 8, 10 and 15	Most Complex

The analysis was done on scores obtained by subjects on all the three categories of figures and also on total score. The results are presented in Tables 22, 23, 24 and 25.

TABLE 22

Mean Scores on 'Most Simple' Figures for the Four Groups
(N-400)

		CREATIVITY	
		High	Low
INTELLIGENCE	High	14.565 (2.50)	15.095 (3.00)
	Low	15.114 (2.66)	15.428 (3.05)
	Total	14.838 (2.60)	15.273 (3.03)

ANALYSIS OF VARIANCE

Source	df	MS	*F*	*p*
Creativity	1	.1780	2.23	n.s.
Intelligence	1	.1944	2.435	n.s.
Interaction	1	.011831	.1482	n.s.
Error	396	.079819		

TABLE 23

Mean Scores on 'Intermediate' Figures for the Four Groups
(N=400)

		CREATIVITY	
		High	Low
INTELLIGENCE	High	16.655 (2.84)	16.649 (2.94)
	Low	16.589 (2.91)	17.381 (3.15)
	Total	16.622 (2.87)	17.035 (3.09)

ANALYSIS OF VARIANCE

Source	df	MS	F	p
Creativity	1	.1545	1.74	n.s.
Intelligence	1	.1109	1.25	n.s.
Interaction	1	.1592	1.79	n.s.
Error	396	.0887		

TABLE 24

Mean Scores on 'Most Complex' Figures for the Four Groups

(N=400)

		CREATIVITY	
		High	Low
INTELLIGENCE	High	19.57 (2.72)	19.31 (3.33)
	Low	19.19 (2.91)	19.61 (2.37)
	Total	19.38 (2.82)	19.47 (2.84)

ANALYSIS OF VARIANCE

Source	df	MS	*F*	*p*
Creativity	1	.006084	.074	n.s.
Intelligence	1	.001296	.016	n.s.
Interaction	1	.146668	1.79	n.s.
Error	396	.0815		

TABLE 25

Mean Scores of Perceptual Simplicity-Complexity for the Four Groups

		CREATIVITY	
		High	Low
INTELLIGENCE	High	3.392 (0.52)	3.445 (0.61)
	Low	3.386 (0.59)	3.552 (0.53)
	Total	3.389 (0.56)	3.503 (0.57)

ANALYSIS OF VARIANCE

Source	df	MS	*F*	*p*
Creativity	1	.011990	3.682	n.s.
Intelligence	1	.0025550	0.783	n.s.
Interaction	1	.003193	0.9805	n.s.
Error	396	.003256212		

The results indicate that on all the three categories of figures the mean scores obtained by the high and the low creative groups do not differ significantly. However, on 'most complex' figures the low creatives show an edge over the high creatives perhaps because high creatives do not even find 'most complex' figures as complex as the low creatives will perceive them. High creatives, as pointed out by Barron, find order in disorder, harmony in disharmony and tolerance for unusual ideas and formulations. They are not immobilised by anxiety in the face of great uncertainty. In short, they find integration where disintegration exists. However, the results may be interpreted with great amount of caution since the test as stated by the author has only the face validity.

Creative Personality is Perceptually Open

The ability to tolerate ambiguity is to accept conflict and tension resulting from polarity (Fromm, 1959), to tolerate inconsistencies and contradictions (Maslow, 1962), to accept the unknown, to be comfortable with the ambiguous, approximate and uncertain. In the present study it denotes those operationally defined qualities as measured by Budner's Tolerance-Intolerance of Ambiguity Scale.

In order to test the hypothesis that the high creatives do not differ significantly from the low creatives on a measure of intolerance of ambiguity analysis of variance was done and results obtained are presented in Table 26.

The results point out that the mean scores on intolerance of ambiguity of the high (63.163) and the low (63.919) creativity groups are not significantly different from one another, although a lesser mean of the high creatives in comparison to the low creatives indicates that the high creatives are less intolerant of ambiguity or in other words more tolerant of ambiguity—a result which has been found consistently by many previous researchers like Raychaudhury (1965), Gust (1964), Barron (1 58), Buel (1965), Goyal (1972) and others. In contrast the low creatives are more intolerant of ambiguity. However, as already stated, the means of the high and the low

TABLE 26

Mean Scores of Intolerance of Ambiguity for the Four Groups
(N=400)

		CREATIVITY	
		High	Low
INTELLIGENCE	High	62.500	63.358
		(8.12)	(7.51)
	Low	63.831	64.409
		(7.29)	(8.45)
	Total	63.163	63.919
		(7.74)	(8.04)

ANALYSIS OF VARIANCE

Source	df	MS	*F*	*p*
Creativity	1	.515524	0.823	n.s.
Intelligence	1	1.418481	2.265	n.s.
Interaction	1	.019600	.0313	n.s.
Error	396	.6261171		

creativity groups do not differ significantly and hence the proposed hypothesis is confirmed.

Comparison of High and Low Creative Groups (based on relative standing on Total Creativity index alone)

Based upon their relative standing on the total creativity index alone high and low creative groups were formed with 108 subjects in each category. In this type of classification, *intelligence was not taken into consideration.* Mean and standard deviations for both the groups on each of the ten independent variables is, presented in Table 28. A test of significance has been used to test the mean difference between the high creative and low creative groups on each variable.

From Table 27 it is apparent that the high creatives and the low creatives differ significantly on intelligence ($t=4.53$; sig. at .01 level). Also the high and the low creatives differ significantly on mechanical reasoning ($t=2.24$; sig. at .05 level) ; economical value ($t=2.03$; sig. at .05 level) ; aesthetic value ($t=2.01$; sig. at .05 level) and religious value ($t=2.93$; sig. at .01 level). These results, therefore, indicate that the above variables could distinguish significantly between the high and the low creative groups.

In the case of theoretical value the mean is higher for the high creatives which shows that the high creatives are relatively higher on theoretical value in comparison to the low creatives. Almost similar conclusion can be drawn for social value for which too the mean is in favour of the high creatives, though the differences are not statistically significant. On the other hand the means of the low creative group on political value and intolerance of ambiguity are relatively higher in comparison to the high creative group indicating thereby that the low creatives are more intolerant of ambiguity and have a slight leaning for personal power, influence and renown.

Discussion

It will be noted from the above that the high creative group is significantly higher on the measure of intelligence than the low creative group. This phenomenon seems to corroborate the earlier findings by different investigators. Roe in a letter to

TABLE 27

Comparison of High and Low Creative Groups on Ten Variables

(Total-Creativity)

Variables	Mean		S.D.		T
	High	Low	High	Low	Value
Intelligence	21.4537	18.3981	4.911	4.997	4.53**
Mech. Reasoning	29.4444	25.9537	11.979	10.872	2.24*
Theoretical Value	45.6574	44.8611	6.073	7.805	0.84
Economical Value	44.8518	42.6667	6.852	8.844	2.03*
Aesthetic Value	31.9074	29.6204	8.586	8.111	2.01*
Social Value	43.1296	42.3981	6.420	8.139	0.73
Political Value	38.5092	39.1111	5.370	7.905	—0.65
Religious Value	32.4630	29.4352	7.517	7.660	2.93**
Simplicity-Complexity	3.3519	3.5185	.569	.619	—2.06*
Intolerance of Ambiguity	62.8055	63.5648	7.636	8.079	—0.71

Note : 1. Sample size for high and low creative groups is 108 each.
2. Degrees of freedom associated with each test are 214.
3a. *at .05 level of significance and
b. **at .01 level of significance.

Kubie (1962) wrote that the level of intelligence of her group was extremely high. Similarly Barron (1969) commenting on the results of the studies done at the Institute of Personality Assessment and Research maintained that "the generalization suggested by these findings is not that intelligence is unrelated to creativity, but rather that individuals of varying degrees of creativity in professions intrinsically creative in character are of quite high measured intelligence. . . ." Similarly, Yamamoto (1964d) found that the high creative group scored higher on the intelligence measure than the low creative group. Gardner (1964) who gave eleven results and the most important of which was that, except for bright children, IQ had a major influence on creativity, also attests to the same phenomenon.

To conclude, the fact remains and is further strengthened by this study that the persons of high creative ability are, by and large, more intelligent than the persons with low creative ability. There is a significant difference between high and low creative groups on a measure of mechanical reasoning. The high creatives perform higher on the mechanical reasoning Test which is designed to test their reasoning ability in the mechanical field and their understanding of mechanical and physical principles in familiar situations. This result shows that the qualities of competence in the specific field and in its related work, on involvement in it and a sensitivity to its requirements are essential in addition to the motivational and personological qualities for greater creativity in the field. Similar point has been made by Maddi (1965) when he argues that needs for both quality and novelty are necessary for creative production. The phenomenon further explains itself from the fact that the ability measured by the Mechanical Reasoning Test may be regarded as one aspect of intelligence, if intelligence is broadly defined.

The Table 27 further indicates that the high creatives are higher on economical value in comparison to the low creatives. The phenomenon is particularly significant in the Indian context since the subjects drawn for the study come from middle class families who have to continuously keep in view the financial limits and economic stringencies. The result is again quite in

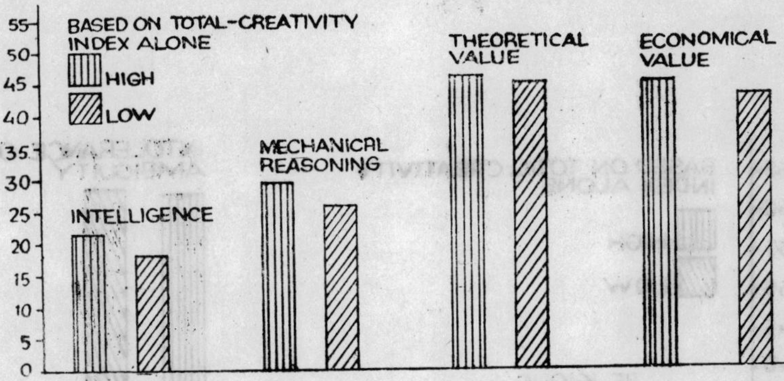

Chart 2

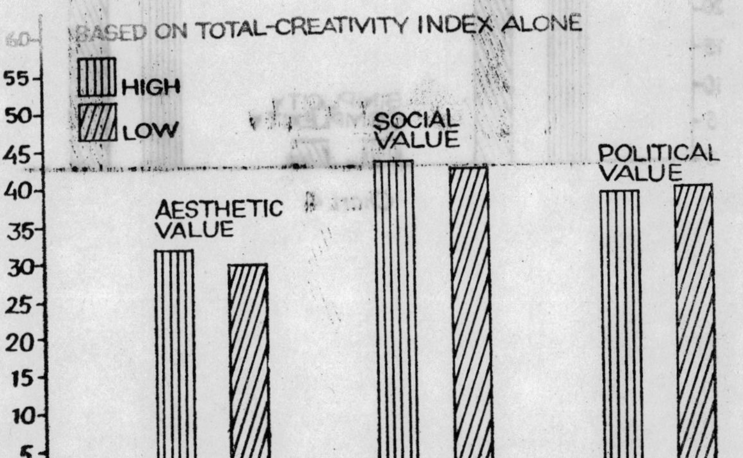

Chart 3

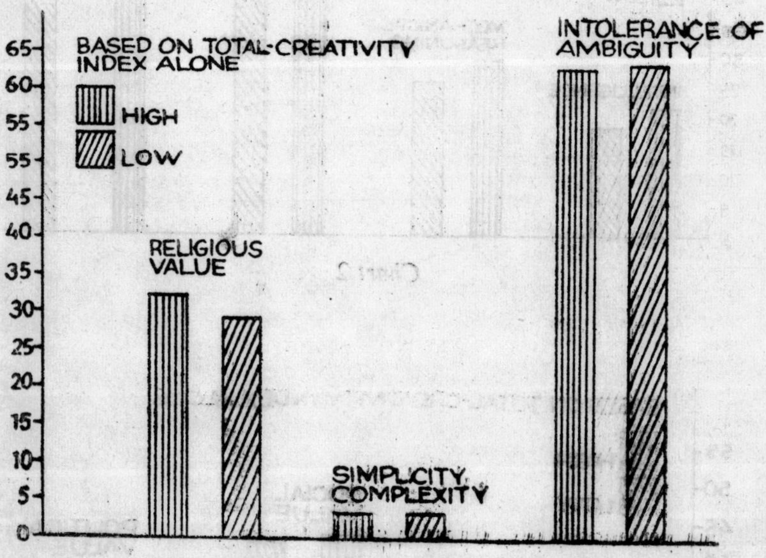
65
60
55
55
45
40
35
30
25
20
15
10
5
0
BASED ON TOTAL-CREATIVITY INDEX ALONE
HIGH
LOW
RELIGIOUS VALUE
SIMPLICITY COMPLEXITY
INTOLERANCE OF AMBIGUITY

Chart 4

tune with the philosophy of the profession itself.

Engineering creativity is primarily characterized through valuable novelty in products (Gregory, 1972). An engineer in certain respects can be equated to the 'economic man' who is characteristically interested in what is useful. Etimologically the word engineering means 'to produce'. To an engineer knowledge is not an end in itself but is simply the raw material from which he fashions structures, machines and processes. Like the 'economic man' who regards unapplied and non-practical knowledge as waste, the engineer also basically insists upon the adjective 'practical'. Engineering, therefore, has rightly been defined as 'the art of making practical application of the knowledge of pure science'. Great feats of engineering and application result from the demands economic men make upon science (Kundu, 1977). Another common economic component of engineering is the 'value of utility' and 'cost consciousness'.

Thus it may be concluded with fair amount of confidence that the economical value is an important variable which differentiates significantly the high creatives from the low creatives.

The mean for high-creativity group on aesthetic value is 31.91, while for the low-creativity group it is 29.62. This shows a positive effect of creativity on aesthetic value. While this result is in conformity with those of Walberg and Welch (1967), MacKinnon (1961) and Paramesh (1972), it does not agree with that of Yamamoto (1963) who obtained no difference between the high and the low-creatives on aesthetic scale.

Another distinctive factor differe. tiating significantly the high and the low-creativity group came out to be the religious value. The mean for high creative group is 32.46 while that of low-creative group it is 29.44. This finding is particularly important in the Indian context where spiritual values are stressed very much, more than anywhere else. Regarding the attitude of adolescents towards religion in India, studies reveal that persons having modern education do not appear to have any unfavourable attitude towards it (Tondon, 1967). Great engineers and scientists of our country were perhaps primarily religious men in their private life. Therefore, it is not surprising that high creatives find more strength and greater inspiration from the lives of great Indian scientists, saints and religious gurus. Higher preference for religious value can be traced in the family tradition and beliefs of the subjects, majority of whom happened to be Punjabis and Sikhs—those who traditionally have strong religious convictions and beliefs. Further the comparison of the high and the low creative groups on the perceptual simplicity-complexity variable evinced statistically significant differences. The *t* ratio worked out to be -2.06 (significant at .05 level of significance). This indicates that the high creatives have a greater appeal for the complex, unfinished and the imperfect. They like asymmetry to symmetry. They find even hazy, complex and subtle drawings or figures quite interesting and, therefore, prefer to investigate them and in the process perceive them as clear, simple and obvious. They have a strong desire to turn disorder into meaning. As opposed to this, the low creatives seek order and simplicity. They don't like asymmetrical, unfinished or vague figures. Hence they perceive even relatively simple, less hazy and less vague drawings as complex, hazy and vague. Similar conclusions have been drawn by Blade (1963) for creative engineers when he said "But more important for creative engineers may be their ability to perceive order from disorder, to find new solutions, to discover through methods of "cut and try", to fancy, imagine and be ingenious."

Correlational Analysis

In order to examine the relationship of one variable to another and to find out the extent to which changes in one variable are accompanied by—or are dependent upon—changes in a second variable Product-Moment Coefficients of Correlation were worked out between the 13 variables. The means and standard deviations of the criterion and predictor variables are presented in the Table 28. Frequency distributions were worked out for criterion (Total Creativity) and ten predictor variables.

TABLE 28

Statistics for Variables

VARIABLES		STATISTICS			
S. No.	Variables	Sample Size	MEAN	S.D. (σ)	Std. Error (σ_e)
1.	Fluency	400	49.563	9.993	.500
2.	Flexibility	400	50.010	10.040	.502
3.	Total Creativity	400	50.022	10.038	.502
4.	Intelligence	400	19.830	5.065	.253
5.	Mech. Reasoning	400	28.032	11.470	.573
6.	Theoretical Value	400	45.500	6.599	.330
7.	Economical Value	400	44.077	7.383	.369

(Contd.)

(Table 28 Contd.)

(1)	(2)	(3)	(4)	(5)	(6)
8.	Aesthetic Value	400	31.190	7.971	.399
9.	Social Value	400	43.055	6.861	.343
10.	Political Value	400	38.675	6.087	.304
11.	Religious Value	400	31.455	7.463	.373
12.	Simplicity-Complexity	400	3.445	.573	.029
13.	Intolerance of Ambiguity	400	63.535	7.915	.396

These are shown in Appendix A : Chart 1 to Chart 11. Inspection of these frequency distributions indicate that they are, in general, normal and that the analyses are being conducted with fairly normal distributions.

Intercorrelations

The intercorrelations for all the 13 variables are shown in Table 29. The significance of these intercorrelations at the .05 and .01 level of significance is also indicated in this Table.

Study of the intercorrelations of the variables discloses that fluency and flexibility are positively and significantly correlated with total creativity. These correlations are very high and significant at .01 level of significance. Fluency and flexibility between themselves are also positively correlated at .01 level of significance. These results are quite in tune with expected lines since the total creativity score in this study is derived by a specific combination of fluency and flexibility scores as obtained from the Purdue Creativity Test. This provides additional strength to the utility and validity of the test used.

Positive and significant correlation is also found between intelligence and total creativity (significant at .01 level of significance). A perusal of the correlational studies done earlier between the measures of creativity and intelligence indicates that the correlations obtained have varied from study to study. Different researchers, however, have different arguments for this phenomenon. In the present study the correlation coefficient between intelligence and total creativity worked out to be .258. This finding is in line with many other important studies done in this potential but most controversial area. Richards, Cline and Needham (1964) have shown that five of Guilford's creativity tests have a median correlation of .40 with the California Test of Mental Maturity. Meer and Stein (1955) found a positive correlation between the measures of creativity and intelligence. MacKinnon (1962) maintained that over the whole range of creativity and intelligence there is, of course, a positive relationship between the two variables. Buhl (1958)

TABLE 29

Intercorrelations of Variables

Variables	Fl.	Flex.	Int.	M.R.	Th. Val.	Eco. Val.	Aes. Val.	Soc. Val.	Pol. Val.	Rel. Val.	Simp.-Comp.	Intol. of Amb.	T. Crea.
Fluency	1.000	.482**	.215**	.124*	—.012	.062	.101*	.036	.004	.063	—057	—.070	.719**
Flexibility		1 000	.226**	.161**	.047	.116*	.061	.018	—063	.112*	—.134**	—.056	.946**
Intelligence			1 000	.414**	—017	.077	.092	—.055	—.117	—.056	—.088	—.070	.258**
Mech. Reas.				1 000	—082	.205**	.154**	—087	—.017	—.090	—.131**	.013	.169**
Theore. Value					1.000	.198**	.045	.401**	.139**	—069	—.069	—.017	.033
Econo. Value						1 000	.137**	.096	.056	—033	—.114*	.019	.116*
Aesth Value							1 000	—.163**	.080	—072	.077	.031	.082
Social Value								1.000	.284**	.175**	—.051	.007	036
Polit. Value									1 000	.125*	—.071	.029	—.046
Relig Value										1 000	—.012	057	.112*

Simpl.-Comp.	1 000	.0065	—.121*
Intolerance of Ambiguity		1.000	—.068
Total Creativity			1.000

Note : 1. Total Creativity (last column/last row) is the criterion variable (T.C.)

2 Only three decimal places retained, rest rounded off.

3a. *at 0 5 level of significance and

b. **at .01 level of significance.

studying engineering creativity pointed out that " . . . an individual with a high mental potential has a greater opportunity to exercise his creative ability."

In fact, many studies have indicated the existence of significant correlations between divergent and convergent thinking. A recent summary of the Minnesota studies of creative behaviour (1958 to 1966) by Torrance (1967) showed that from a total of 178 coefficients of correlation between measures of intelligence and a total or composite measure of creative thinking ability the median *r* is .20 which explains adequately the correlation of .258 found in the present study between intelligence and total creativity. Intelligence and mechanical reasoning in this study are positively and significantly correlated with each other ; the correlation being very high (.414) and significant at .01 level of significance. This result is quite in agreement with the reported nature of the Mechanical Reasoning Test whereby the ability measured by this test has been regarded by its authors as one aspect of intelligence, if intelligence is broadly defined.

Intelligence is also found significantly correlated in this study with political value ; the correlation is negative and significant only at .05 level of significance.

The results also show that correlations of theoretical value with economical, social and political values are all significant at .01 level of significance. Economical value is also correlated with total creativity at .05 level of significance. These correlations found in this study can be explained in the perspective of an engineer—his approach to problem-solving and the varieties of social, economical and political constraints with which the engineers have to compromise for their creative problem-solving. As a matter of fact engineering is hedged with limitations. In solving engineering problems these limits are generally very restrictive and involve public or governmental policies ; the limits of cost, marketing, time, auxiliary services available ; and restrictive codes, union labour laws and other limits. Generally the creative engineer perhaps seeks a solution which solves the problem within the given limits. The engineer is a problem solver to satisfy the wants of others. This is in distinction to the creative scientist, who often creates for himself in searching for his ideas of truth and reality and for understanding. Thus the engineer's freedom is restricted in a predefined manner to a much greater extent than is the freedom of the scientist. However, within these boundary conditions and limits imposed by the assignments there may be many freedoms of action that give the engineer an opportunity to create. These outcomes of engineering creativity are all results of societal, economical and political values in which the engineer solves his assigned problems. Thus the pursuit for unknown by an engineer has always a socio-economic and political relevance and feasibility attached to it.

Other positive and significant correlations are found between economical and aesthetic value and social and political value. Aesthetic value is negatively but significantly correlated with social value. These relationships are in line with the inter-correlations given in the manual of the test. Religious value, besides being significantly correlated with social and political values, is also positively and significantly correlated with total creativity. The correlation is, however, only significant at .05 level of significance. The correlation between total creativity and perceptual simplicity-complexity is also significant at .05 level of significance. The negative correlation obtained in this case indicates that the creative engineers perceive order in disorder. They have a greater appeal for the unfinished and the imperfect. Even irregular, subtle and hazy figures or drawings are perceived by them as simple, obvious and clear. Intolerance of ambiguity is negatively correlated with total creativity but the resulting correlation coefficient is statistically insignificant. The negative correlation indicates that the creative engineers are tolerant of ambiguity, i.e. they have the capacity to tolerate inconsistencies and contradictions and be comfortable with the ambiguous, approximate and uncertain.

Multiple Regression Analysis

Torrance (1967) presents huge amount of data which impresses one with futility of doing simple correlation studies of the relationship between measure of intelligence and creative thinking ability". So, it was considered useful to go beyond correlational analysis presented in the previous section, (where correlations were found between two variables at a time and the prediction was made of one variable Y from X). But actual relationship between measured things in psychology and education, as remarked by Guilford (1950), are by no means so simple, as that one variable is found associated with or dependent upon, more than one variable at the same time. On the basis of this observation, it will be readily admitted that creative performance, whether high or low is not entirely dependent upon or is not only a function of intelligence alone. Perhaps, other variables also contribute their share to the prediction of creative performance. In the light of the above remarks the following discussion will seek to provide an answer to the following questions :

1. What is the extent to which creative performance or total creativity can be predicted by the ten variables : 1. Intelligence 2. Mechanical Reasoning 3. Theoretical Value 4. Economical Value 5. Aesthetic Value 6. Social Value 7. Political Value 8. Religious Value 9. Perceptual Simplicity-Complexity 10. Intolerance of Ambiguity, in combination and as a team ?
2. What combination of the tests used in this study will give a relatively better prediction of creative performance i.e., total creativity.
3. What is the contribution of each variable to the multiple correlation or more specifically what percentage of variance in the dependent variable is accounted for by each of the ten predictor variables mentioned above.

The regression equation for predicting the total creativity was worked out for the meaningful predictor variables. When more than one predictor variable is available the problem of combining them to provide the most effective selection arises. There are a great many possible ways of combining scores, but the most generally useful one is to make a linear combination of these scores. This means for each test some weight is determined. These weights, which are applied to the separate test scores to obtain the test prediction of the criteria are called regression weights and the equation based on them is the multiple regression equation for predicting the criterion scores (Thomson, 1956).

In order to predict the creativity step-up Multiple Regression Analysis was undertaken. At each step one variable was added and a multiple correlation was determined and its significance was tested by *F* test. The process of adding the variable was continued till this ratio becomes insignificant i.e. when multiple R is insignificant at .05 level of significance. After determining the regression equation, significance of increment due to the addition of each variable, was tested.

In this regression analysis, in all ten variables namely intelligence, religious value, economical value, simplicity-complexity, aesthetic value, intolerance of ambiguity, political value, mechanical reasoning, social value and theoretical value were considered for the prediction of creativity. The multiple correlation coefficients, their significance, the significance in the increase of multiple correlation coefficients at each step and degrees of freedom are presented in Table 30.

In the regression analysis the variables of fluency and flexibility have not been considered since they are themselves constituents of the criterion variable : Total Creativity.

Table 30 presents information for each independent variable at the conclusion of the final step. Presented here are Multiple R, the R square and the increment in R square from the value of the previous step. Simple *r* is the correlation between the independent variable and the dependent variable, i.e. the criterion variable in in this case. The *F* is the ratio of the two mean sum of squares.

During the analysis a multiple R was determined between the criterion variable and the linear combination of independent variables. In this way the multiple R between the criterion and the variable intelligence at first step and linear combination of intelligence, religious value at second step were found significant. The value of multiple R at the third step is only 2.061

TABLE 30

Stepwise Multiple Regression Analysis

Dependent Variable : Total Creativity

Variables	Simple r	Multiple Correlation (R)	R Square	Increment	*F* Value	df
Intelligence	.258	.258	.067		15.845	1,398
Religious Value	.112	.288	.083	(.01610)	8.452 (6.97)	2,397 (1,397)
Economical Value	.116	.306	.094	(.01058)	2.061 (4.62)	3,396 (1,396)
Simplicity-Complexity	—.121	.318	.101	(.00734)	3.465 (3.23)	4,395 (1,395)
Aesthetic Value	.082	.324	.105	(.00399)	2.119 (1.76)	5,394 (1,394)
Intolerance of Ambiguity	—.068	.330	.109	(.00376)	1.715 (1.65)	6,393 (1,393)

Political Value	—.046	.334	.111	(.00269)	1.735 (1.18)	7,392 (1,392)
Mechanical Reasoning	.169	.337	.114	(.00232)	1.235 (1.02)	8,391 (1,391)
Social Value	.036	.340	.116	(.00191)	0.492 (0.84)	9,390 (1,390)
Theoretical Value	.033	.340	.116	(.00029)	0.128 (0.13)	10,389 (1,389)

which is insignificant at .05 level of significance ; it is due to higher inter-correlations between economical value and aesthetic value and simplicity-complexity. Whereas its correlation with criterion is low. However, while testing the increment due to the addition of each variable it was found that the three variables viz : intelligence, religious value and economical value turned out to be significant. The multiple R was also found significant after the addition of the fourth variable i.e. simplicity-complexity but its increment in R^2 was found insignificant at .05 level of significance. Therefore, only three variables namely intelligence, religious value and economical value were taken into consideration for deciding final prediction equation. The regression equation thus obtained is as follows :

$$Y = A + \beta_1 X_1 + \beta_2 X_2 + \beta_3 X_3$$

Where :

A — intercept

β_1, β_2 & β_3—regression coefficients of intelligence, religious value and economical value respectively

Y — total creativity

X_1— intelligence

X_2— religious value

X_3— economical value

in this case :

A = 28.10

β_1 = .51

β_2 = .18

β_3 = .14

Therefore :

$$Y = 28.10 + .51X_1 + .18X_2 + .14X_3$$

The results, therefore, indicate that in this study the single best predictor of creativity is intelligence, which is positively related to creativity i.e. individual's high on creativity are high on intelligence also. This result obtained in the present study seems to be echoed in the statement made by Gregory (1972) that for individuals to be creative in engineering they must generally have an I.Q. of 115 or greater. Guilford (1972) too maintained that "high status in cognition is a necessary condition for high status in divergent production, but it is not a sufficient condition." The results of the present study are in agreement with the results reported by Mednick and Andrews (1967) and by Ginsberg and Whittemore (1968), who also found a positive linear relationship between creativity and intelligence throughout the range. In fact, many studies have indicated the existence of significant correlations between divergent and convergent thinking (Raina, 1969). Therefore, it may be concluded that intelligence is perhaps necessary condition for creative performance which provides the vocabulary to be sorted and the means of selection (Kubie, 1958).

The second and third factors in order of importance are religious value and economical value which are also positively correlated to total creativity, meaning thereby that individuals high on creativity are high on religious and economical values. Other factors are found to be statistically insignificant. Although the addition of each test raises the multiple correlation, some do so only very little ; and our caution in ordering the tests in accordance with the magnitude of the criterion correlation makes it probable, though not certain, that the comparatively useless tests will be the later ones. Therefore Thomson (1956) suggests that one can at each stage of the calculation pause and see whether the test we have just added makes a significant addition to the multiple correlation. Is the rise statistically significant ? This has been done by analysis of variance (Lindquist, 1940).

Although the increment due to the addition of variable simplicity-complexity is not statistically significant but its multiple R between criterion variable and intelligence, religious value, economical value, simplicity-complexity is found significant. Hence one could meaningfully use any one combination of the factors depending upon the time and resources available. The larger the number of factors included, the better the coverage of total creativity.

TABLE 31

Varimax Rotated Factor Matrix

Variables	Factor 1	Factor 2	Factor 3	Factor 4	Factor 5
Total Creativity	.58646	.06051	.36960	.01845	.27115
Intelligence	**.72590**	—.09837	—.01801	—.01723	—.17772
Mechanical Reasoning	**.73340**	—.06682	—.12659	.04760	.18496
Theoretical Value	—.03576	**.77898**	—.19706	—.00772	—.15031
Economical Value	.37728	.45131	—.25301	.11144	.20620
Aesthetic Value	.25614	.07035	—.08553	**.80115**	.14751
Social Value	—.10743	**.72423**	.27780	—.21477	—.08322
Political Value	—.09597	**.51096**	.31242	.17363	.27576
Religious Value	—.01847	.01895	**.86449**	—.04319	.08404
Simplicity-Complexity	—.35906	—.16909	.06279	**.61797**	—.24773
Intolerance of Ambiguity	—.00536	—.05329	.06726	—.01049	**.83042**

Factor Analysis

In order to find out the important factors contributing to engineering creativity, Varimax Rotated Factor Analysis has been done. The Table 31 gives the Varimax Rotated Factor Matrix for all the eleven variables namely Total Creativity, Intelligence, Mechanical Reasoning, Theoretical Value, Economical Value, Aesthetic Value, Social Value, Political Value, Religious Value, Simplicity-Complexity and Intolerance of Ambiguity.

As indicated in the Table, Factor 1 is dominated by the variables like intelligence and mechanical reasoning which can be termed as an 'Intellective Factor.' In Factor 2 variables like theoretical value, social value and political value are contributing more than any other variables and this factor hence can be named as 'Values Factor.' In Factor 3, only the variable religious value has a larger regression coefficient. Therefore, Factor 3 can be named as a factor of 'Religious Value.' In Factor 4 the variables aesthetic value and simplicity-complexity have considerable contribution. Hence this factor can be termed as a 'Stylistic Factor.' In Factor 5 only the variable intolerance of ambiguity has the maximum contribution. This factor, therefore, may be named as 'Factor of Openness.' These five factors in all contribute 61.8% of variance of the total information gathered through the eleven variables. Table 32 gives the percentage of variance accounted for by each of the factors.

TABLE 32

Eigenvalue and Percentage of Variance accounted for by each of the five Factors

Factor	Eigenvalue	Percentage of Variance	Cumulative percentage
1.	1.80360	16.4	16.4
2.	1.69388	15.4	31.8
3.	1.19902	10.9	42.7
4.	1.10166	10.0	52.7
5.	1.00286	9.1	61.8

As indicated in Table 32 Factor 1 gives 16.4% of variance, Factor 2 : 15.4%, Factor 3 : 10.9%, Factor 4 : 10.0% and Factor 5 : 9.1% of variance.

Intellective Factors Necessary but not Sufficient

The results suggest that the psychological constitution of the creative engineer and the assessment of his creative potential cannot merely rely on singular intellectual traits but must also include cognitive styles and personality variables. Thus the cognitive factors which, though, are essential to creativity, function not in isolation, but rather in relation to a total personality system. Bloom (1963), while engaged in an extensive research of the cognitive dimensions associated with scientific creativity, concluded that "personality and motivational factors are at least as important as aptitude in determining performance." Hence it may be concluded from the present study that to predict engineering creativity to a high degree, one must get at a large number of different characteristics both intellective and non-intellective collectively to account for the major variance in the total creative performance.

CHAPTER VII

Summary, Conclusions, Educational Implications and Recommendations

Summary

The major objective of the present study was to compare quantitatively significant differences between high and low creative groups on certain measures of mechanical reasoning, value orientations, perceptual simplicity-complexity and intolerance of ambiguity. The psychometric instruments administered to the subjects included (1) Purdue Creativity Test, Form H (2) Culture Fair Intelligence Test, Scale 3 (3) Mechanical Reasoning Test (4) Value Test (5) Perceptual Simplicity-Complexity Test and (6) The Budner Tolerance-Intolerance of Ambiguity Scale.

The population of this study consisted of 522 students specializing in mechanical engineering branch of all the diploma-level engineering institutions for boys in the union territory of Delhi. In the final analysis, however, a total of 400 subjects were studied for whom data on all the variables under investigation were available.

In order to compose groups that would constitute the four possible combinations of high and low creativity and intelligence, the index scores for creativity and intelligence were dichotomised at their median and called 'high' if they fell in the upper half of the distribution, 'low' if they fell in the lower half. Thus, all cases in the sample were utilized, rather than just upper and lower extremes. The subjects were, therefore, classified into four sub-groups namely the High Creative-High Intelligence, the High Creative-Low Intelligence, the Low Creative-High Intelligence and the Low Creative-Low Intelligence based on their joint standing on the creativity and intelligence index scores. For the comparison of these four sub-groups by the 2×2 analysis of variance technique, the scores on mechanical reasoning, theoretical value, economical value, aesthetic value, social value, political value, religious value, perceptual simplicity-complexity - (combined ; on 'most simple' figures ; 'intermediate' figures and on 'most complex' figures) and intolerance of ambiguity were treated individually.

In addition, a comparison of high and low creative groups formed on the basis of their relative standing on total creativity index alone (with 108 subjects in each category) was also made. In this type of classification intelligence was not taken into consideration. A test of significance was used to test the mean difference between the high creative and low creative groups on each variable.

Product moment correlation coefficients were computed to establish intercorrelations between criterion (total creativity) and predictors (other variables).

In order to predict the creativity step-up multiple regression analysis was also undertaken. After determining the regression equation significance of increment due to the addition of each variable, was tested. The three variables namely intelligence, religious value and economical value were ultimately taken into consideration for deciding the final prediction equation.

Finally, Varimax Rotated Factor Analysis was done to find out the important factors contributing to engineering creativity.

Conclusions

The conclusions of this study are presented according to the order of presentation employed in the previous chapters.

A. Following results were drawn based on analysis of variance :

1. Statistically significant differences were found between the high and the low creativity groups on the Mechanical Reasoning Ability Test indicating thereby a positive effect of creativity on mechanical reasoning. A highly significant effect was seen in the case of intelligence but the interaction effect was insignificant.
2. Results pointed out that the groups were homogeneous so far as theoretical value was concerned. No significant effect was seen in the case of intelligence either, and interaction effect was also insignificant.
3. The results explicitly indicated a positive and significant effect of creativity on economical value. The effect of intelligence and creativity-intelligence interaction remained insignificant.
4. The mean scores on aesthetic value of the high and the low creativity groups were not significantly different from one another, although there was a slight tendency in favour of a positive effect of creativity on aesthetic value. Further, no significant effect was seen in the case of intelligence and interaction effect was insignificant.
5. The results on social value showed no significant effect for both creativity and intelligence. Interaction effect was also insignificant.
6. On political value the high creative group and the low creative group did not differ significantly from one another. Again, no significant effect was seen in the case of intelligence and interaction effect was insignificant.
7. The mean scores on religious value of the high and the low creativity groups were although not significantly different from one another there was a tendency in favour of a positive effect of creativity on religious value. No significant effect was seen in the case of

intelligence, and interaction effect too was insignificant.

8. The high and the low creative groups did not differ significantly on three categories of figures of varying complexity. However, the results pointed out that the high creatives had a greater appeal for the complex, unfinished and the imperfect.

9. The results showed no significant differences on a scale of intolerance of ambiguity. A lesser mean of the high creatives, however, indicated that the high creatives were more tolerant of ambiguity.

B. In another type of classification based on the subject's relative standing on the total creativity index alone (without taking intelligence into consideration) high and low creative groups were compared on all the ten independent variables, Results obtained from this analysis are as follows :

1. High and low creatives differed significantly on intelligence, mechanical reasoning, economical value, aesthetic value, and religious value.
2. In the case of theoretical value and social value the means were in favour of the high creatives although the differences were not statistically significant.
3. Perceptual simplicity-complexity variable further evidenced statistically significant differences indicating that the high creatives had a greater appeal for the complex, unfinished and the imperfect.
4. Results indicated that the high creatives were more tolerant of ambiguity in comparison to the low creatives.

C. A study of intercorrelations of variables disclosed following relationships between the variables :

1. Positive and significant correlation was found between intelligence and total creativity. The correlation coefficient worked out to be .258 (sig. at .01 level).
2. Mechanical reasoning, economical value, religious value and perceptual simplicity-complexity were significantly correlated to total creativity.
3. Intolerance of ambiguity was negatively correlated to

total creativity indicating that the creative engineers had the capacity to tolerate inconsistencies and contradictions and were comfortable with the ambiguous, approximate and uncertain. However, the correlation coefficient was statistically insignificant.

D. The results of the Multiple Regression Analysis indicated the following :

The single best predictor of creativity was intelligence. The second and third factors in order of importance were religious value and economical value. Multiple R between criterion variable and intelligence, religious value, economical value, simplicity-complexity was also found significant, The final regression equation worked out to be :

$Y = 28.10 + .51\ X_1 + .18\ X_2 + .14\ X_3$

Y = total creativity

X_1 = intelligence

X_2 = religious value

X_3 = economical value

E. Varimax Rotated Factor Analysis yielded following five factors :

Factor 1 was an 'Intellective Factor' dominated by variables like intelligence and mechanical reasoning. Factor 2 was termed as a 'Values Factor' in which variables like theoretical, social and political value contributed more than any other variables. In factor 3, only the variable religious value had a larger regression coefficient. Therefore, Factor 3 was named as a 'Factor of Religious Value.' Factor 4 turned out to be a 'Stylistic Factor' with considerable contribution from variables like aesthetic value, and simplicity-complexity, while Factor 5 with maximum contribution of the variable intolerance of ambiguity was a Factor of Openness.

The results obtained in this study, therefore, indicate that the intellective factors do not, in and of themselves, account for differences in creative ability. These intellective factors seem to be a necessary—but not sufficient—ingredient of creativity since they function not in isolation, but rather in relation to a total personality system of needs, attitudes, motivations, values, goals and emotions. The stylistic, motivational and personality characteristics along with cognitive factors, therefore, operate as important determinants in the realization of creative potentialities of young engineers. Hence it may be concluded that innovative performance of creative engineers is a function of a complex interaction among such factors as personality structure, environmental influences and cognitive capacities.

Educational Implications

Engineering is the profession in which khowledge is applied with judgment for the progressive well-being of mankind. The phrases "with judgment" and "progressive well-being of mankind" involve more than "know-how", more than craftsmanship. They involve value judgments. They involve social decisions. They involve leadership in what should be done as well as in what could be done. They involve moral responsibility—a moral responsibility for the direction taken by our civilization and for the sort of lives we live in it.

The aim of engineering education, therefore, must be to prepare the students for a professionally productive life. As practitioners engineers should recognise problems, diagnose them, and find solutions. The technical and technological aspects of a problem should be considered, as well as the cultural, social, legal and economic implications. An engineer should be fully cognizant of a larger system of which his problem is a sub-system and should also evaluate the effects the solution will have on the environment. During the solution of a problem, attention must be paid to all its ramifications, scientific, technical, economic, sociological, psychological, aesthetic etc. When compromises have to be made, these compromises must be based on the understanding of the relations of the problem to the total environment, natural resources, users, etc. so that important effects will not be neglected or compromised. To attack a problem in this manner represents, obviously, an intensive intellectual effort, and it seems highly probable that the attitude of the engineer and the character of his methodology play a greater role in it than the amount of his factual knowledge.

Innovations in engineering education are hard to come by. It is easier to introduce new subject matter or to add new courses into the curriculum than to develop new ways and techniques of teaching. Teaching engineers to define problems or to be aware of areas where something is wrong may not be enough. The innovative engineer must have the ability to generate a multitude of hypotheses or ask many questions which direct him or someone else to investigate constructive measures for changing or correcting perceived inadequacies.

Along with an originality factor characteristic of the creative engineer are various fluency factors of several kinds, such as flow of ideas, flow of associations, and flow of expressions for stating ideas or solutions. There are also several kinds of flexibilities that make up the intellectual characteristics of the creative man. There are likewise some very well-defined motivational characteristics of scientific and engineering creativity. The design engineer who is regarded as creative tends to be more autonomous than others, puts a premium on independence and freedom, and is likely to avoid situations in which others try to dominate or coerce him.

Other motivational characteristics include persistency liking to think, liking to toy with ideas, continual searching for a variety of input experiences, preference for complexity and tolerance for ambiguity. Creative personality is perceptually "open". This implies a resistance to premature judgment. Unfortunately, much of our engineering training and many pressures of our contemporary society deliberately direct us towards immediacy for critical judgment. Faced with something new or different, the engineer searches for flaws, for signs of weakness, or for areas of possible failure.

Too much of our engineering training only emphasises the evaluative behaviour of critically judging what is wrong, and students are too frequently taught to converge upon the one right or acceptable way for correcting it. Our selection system, curriculum, methods of teaching, instructional technology or text books are not in consonance with the development of this human asset. The organisation of our engineering schools, our curriculum offerings and our textbooks pay homage to the same God of conformity and even the selection system emphasises the convergent abilities at the cost of divergent abilities, independent thinking and independent judgment. In the light of new demands and the changes which have taken place in the practice and theory of professional engineering the educational system has far to go. A variety of pilot ventures can be established in several schools to try new techniques in fostering creativity. Illustrations of the variety of approaches can be :

1. Developing creative thinking characteristics.
2. Developing creative personality and motivational characteristics.
3. Overcoming emotional hinderances and blocks to the creative processes.
4. Sensing the unknowns and launching creative ventures therein.
5. Developing special instructional media for creativity.
6. Modifying existing testing materials.
7. Experimenting with related educational techniques such as inquiry training ; discovery methods etc. for fostering creativity.
8. Utilizing recent research findings on creativity.
9. Encouraging creativity workshops for teachers.
10. Developing engineering instructional materials for creativity programmes.

These approaches coupled with other suggestions that have been made, could make a major contribution toward improving the environment for creativity in our engineering institutions.

Recommendations for Further Study

On the basis of the over-view of studies and the gaps found during the process of research reported in this thesis, following are some of the potential areas which need attention and further study :

(a) A study of the process of creativity in engineering will be helpful in judging whether creativity is field-specific. During the present investigation it was found that there is no suitable test for studying creativity in the field of engineering especially in the Indian settings. Therefore, there is a need to develop instruments for studying creativity in different branches of engineering.

(b) The present study, as already stated, has been done with technician engineers ; similar studies can be conducted with graduate engineers. Students of other branches of engineering can also form the sample for studies.

(c) Teaching methods and techniques probably play an important role in the development of creativity. In this context it will be worthwhile to undertake some studies for developing instructional strategies on the basis of findings reported in this study to judge the teachability of creativity with engineers.

(d) Another area that needs attention of future researchers is that of inner experiences and autistic thinking as related to creativity in scientists, engineers and artists. The relationship of stylistic variables and creativity can be further studied using other tools for the purpose.

(e) Attemps may also be made to select a few polytechnic centres in the country to develop engineering curriculum for nurturing creativity and then testing its effectiveness.

Apart from the above some more related areas of investigation are listed below :

(i) Relationship or creative thinking to psychomotor ability, mechanical reasoning ability and vocational attitude of engineering students.

(ii) Factors related to success in technical jobs.

(iii) Organisational factors affecting engineering creativity.

(iv) The prediction of engineering performance with biographical information.

(v) Personality characteristics associated with engineering creativity.

(vi) Personal and environmental determiners of mechanical ingenuity.

(vii) Comparative study of creativity among male and female engineering students.

(viii) Study of differential effectiveness of few methods of fostering engineering creativity.

(ix) Comparison of motor-creativity with verbal and figural creativity.

(x) Effects of on-the-job training for teachers on the creative production of students.

(xi) Religious affiliation, socio-economic status and engineering creativity.

CHAPTER VIII

The Training of Creative Thinking

During rainy season rain water after saturating the upper crust of the earth rushes to low-lying areas. This excessive flow of unchannelized water at times not only causes devastating floods bringing untold miseries to millions of people, but also ultimately gets converted itself into saline water of the sea which cannot even quench the thirst of a thirsty. If on the other hand this excess water is properly channelized it becomes a source of prosperity to the country. Similar is the case with creativity. Creativity is a natural endowment to the human being which if fostered, developed and effectively utilized can take the form of new approaches to traditional problems or contribute to genuine innovation and change in a product, process or technique.

The prime mover of this change in the increasingly technical society of today is an engineer who has to apply knowledge with judgment for the progressive well-being of mankind. The aim of engineering education, therefore, should be to foster appropriate attitudes, strengthen innate abilities and teach systematic creative problem-solving techniques for a professionally productive life. Engineers in their careers as practitioners have to recognise problems, diagnose them, and find their solutions. In arriving at these solutions the engineer has to consider the technical and technological aspects of the problem, as well as the social, cultural, legal and economic implications. During the problem-solving process the engineer should be aware of the limitations of resources, feasibility, fabricability, efficiency and cost of converting an idea into physical reality. To attack a problem in this manner represents an intensive intellectual effort, an ability to generate a multitude of hypotheses or ask many questions which direct him to investigate constructive measures for changing or correcting perceived inadequacies.

Today our engineering education, for most part, emphasizes mastery of the known. Great stress is laid on the evaluative behaviour of judging critically what is wrong. Very little in fact is done to prepare students to cope effectively with the unknown and ambiguous. They are tought to converge at one right or acceptable answer. The admission criteria, curriculum, methods of teaching, instructional techniques or text books fail to foster creative growth ; more often than not they stifle the imaginations and creative capabilities of students. In the light of new demands and enormously complex challenges posed to the engineering profession by problems regarding population explosion, environmental pollution, automation and tremendous scientific advance in the fields of manufacturing processes and products the educational system has far to go.

It is quite natural to ask whether there are some means of developing the creative potential. Can the educational system develop, nurture and achieve a truly creativity-stimulating environment ? Is creativity simply a result of preparation, incubation, inspiration and verification or it can be learned ? Torrance (1967) states that the old myth that creativity is the function of superior genes and 'talent will come out' has been exploded. Now the researchers and theorists have established that every individual is creative in a greater or lesser degree and that the development of creativity cannot be left to chance. In America the attempts to train and develop creative thinking have become very popular (Singh, 1976). During the last two or three decades interest in deliberate training of creative thinking has grown enormously. Many universities have been offering courses in creative problem solving. Many engineering and business companies and corporations are having creative problem-solving programmes for their engineers and management personnel.

Studies on the possibility of improving creativity by deliberate attempts have shown encouraging success (Singh, 1976). It is as foolish to say that the process of creative thought cannot be taught as to say that medicine or engineering cannot be taught (Crawford, 1954). In a rapidly changing society of day, particularly in a developing country like India, the critical role of creative innovation cannot be overemphasised. What are the various methods or techniques of training creative thinking which have been used successfully in engineering concerns and institutions ? One of the earliest courses in creative thinking dates back to 1930s when Crawford for the first time evolved simple but an effective means of generating creative ideas—*attribute listing.* In Crawford's own words : "Each time we take a step, we do it by changing an attribute or a quality of something, or else by applying that same quality or attribute to some other thing." While using this method the teacher may ask students to itemise important attributes of a product. Each attribute thus listed can now be considered as a source of potential change or improvement. By identifying and systematically changing the attributes students learn to improve objects, materials, manufacturing processes, cost and marketability of the product.

Another technique quite similar to 'attribute listing' procedure is *morphological synthesis* in which students are required to list as many characteristics as possible of the given problem and also list specific values for each. Taking one value of each characteristic at a time several possible combinations are worked out. Using this technique large variety of ideas in a short span of time can be produced to change or modify an object or gadget. It is likely that some of these combinations prove useful in bringing out a surprisingly new product.

In America a variety of methods and strategies have been employed to train and develop creative thinking in students. Two of these methods namely 'Brainstorming' (Osborn, 1963) and 'Synectics' (Gordon, 1961) have been found to be most effective. In the words of Vernon the main aim of brainstorming is "to facilitate the expression of the preconscious imagination in a group situation, by deferring conscious critical evaluation." In this method students are encouraged to produce a large number of ideas freely without any inhibition. It is based on the premise that greater the number of ideas produced greater are the chances of finding useful ones. In addition students in this method also try to combine two or more of the ideas for getting newer ideas. An effective brainstorming session is one in which participants do not criticize even the most far-fetched ideas for solving a particular problem. On the other hand students are rather encouraged and also reinforced for spontaneous, free and uninhibited idea productions.

The theory of synectics draws its inspiration from the fact that best ideas occur to may people when conscious thinking is not being done by them about the problem. It is the period of 'incubation' during which inspiration comes about. Synectics endeavours to invoke the preconscious by encouraging oscillation of the problem solving mind between rational consideration of the actual problem and a search for non rational analysis. The more far fetched the analysis the better. This technique follows an approach based on direct analogy or personal analogies, therefore everyone can communicate easily according to his experiences even within a group of people having different backgrounds. The methods of synectics in simplified form can be fruitfully utilized for stimulating the imaginations of students in schools.

Another approach which is comparatively new and has good potential is that of 'Bionics'. In this approach structure, functions and mechanisms of animals and plants are carefully studied. The information thus obtained is then used to gain design information for analogous man-made systems. It is hoped that through this approach bionicists will be able to design machines and systems having better sensitivity, maneou-everability and adaptability which will work with greater precision and economy.

There are many other programmes and techniques which have been developed and used in various institutions, manufacturing industries and business organizations for the training of creativity. Morphological Synthesis, Checklist procedure, Productive Thinking Programme (Covington, Crutchfield and Davies (1966), Idea Books (Myres and Torrance, 1964, 1965a, 1965b, 1966a, 1966b), Thinking Creativity (Davis and Houtman) are only a few to enumerate here.

It may therefore, be argued with fair amount of confidence that there lies a gap between the creative and productive thinking potential endowed in each person and his creative and productive thinking performance. One of the aims of education should be to narrow this gap considerably by appropriate training techniques. Methods and procedures should be designed to make the students think independently for productive and innovative solutions to problems in the schools and colleges. Torrance (1972) as referred by Raina (1973) found that 72% of the total number of 142 studies dealing with various ways of teaching creativity have demonstrated success in the deliberate development of creative ability. Thus the studies on the possibility of improving creativity by deliberate attempts have shown encouraging success (Singh, 1976).

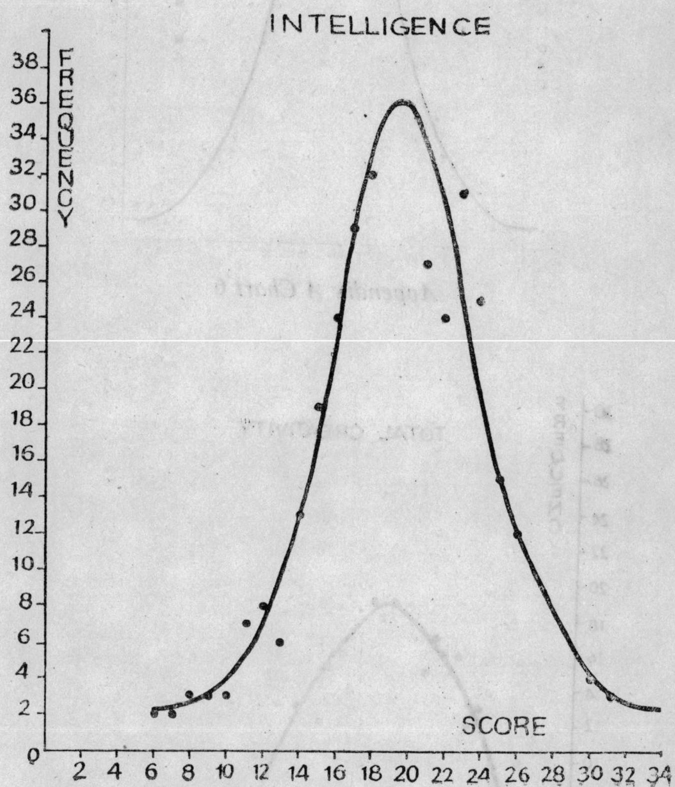

Appendix A Chart 5

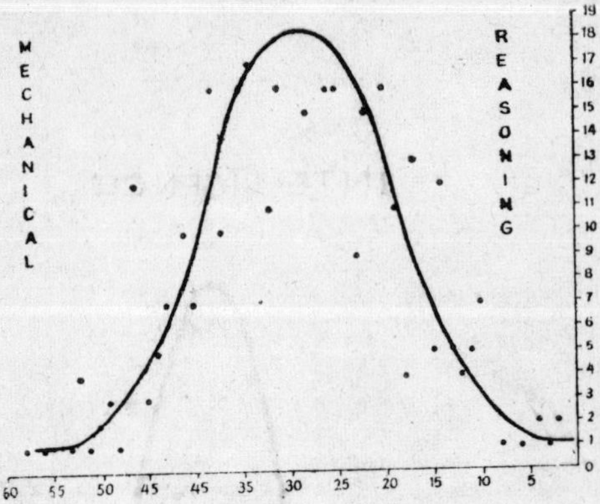

Appendix A Chart 6

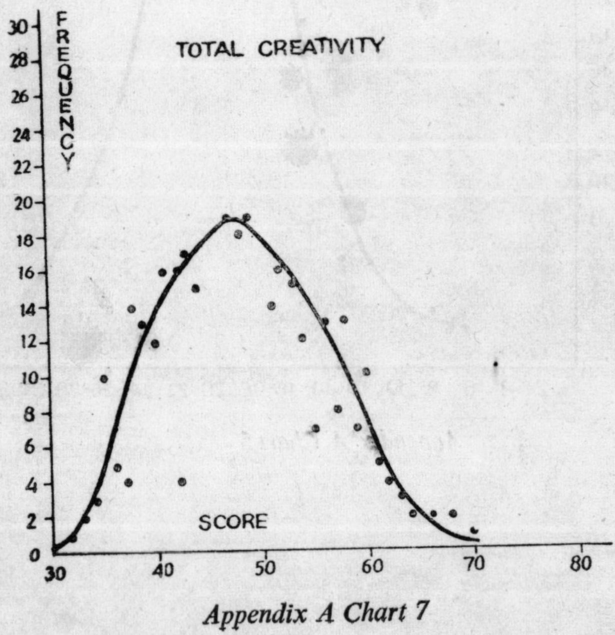

Appendix A Chart 7

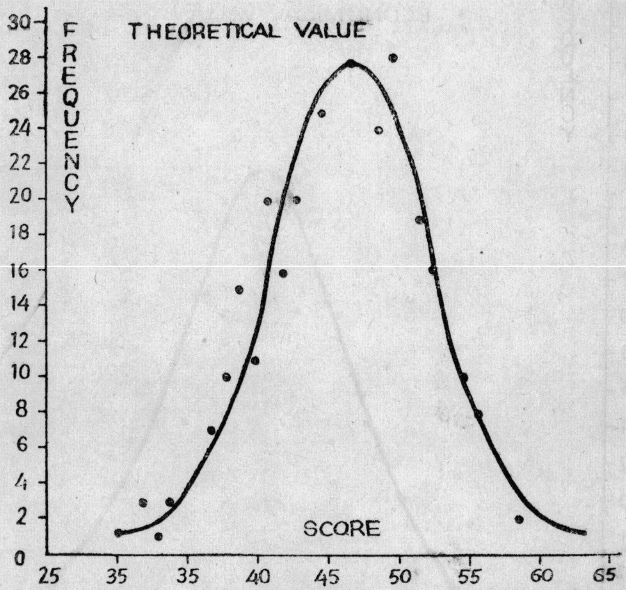

Appendix A Chart 8

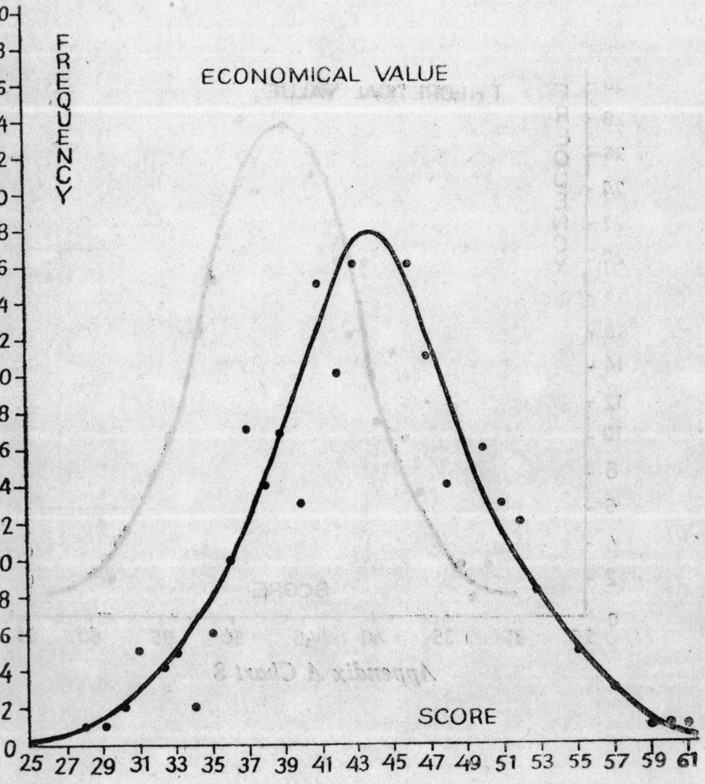

Appendix A Chart 9

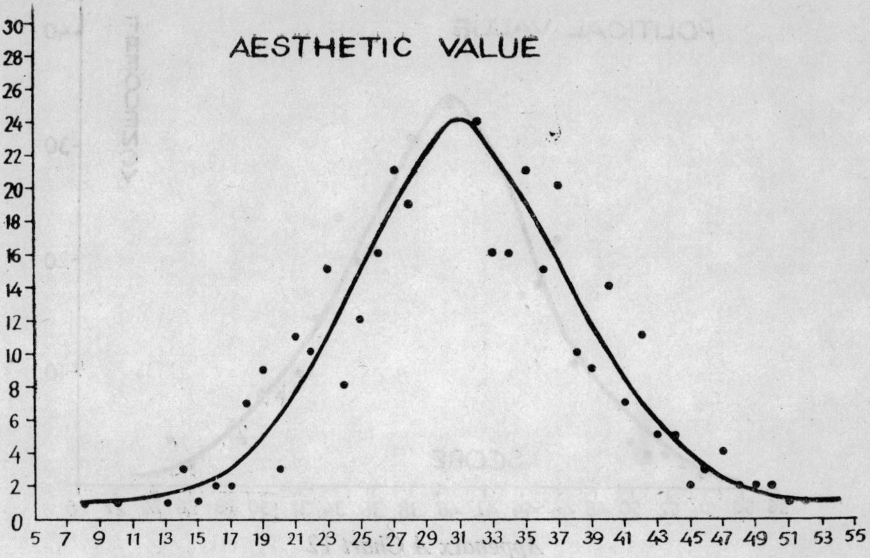

Appendix A Chart 10

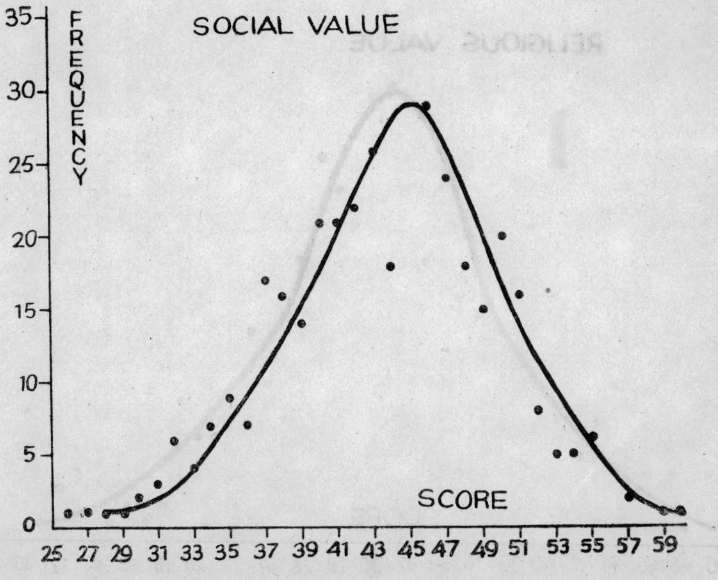

Appendix A Chart 11

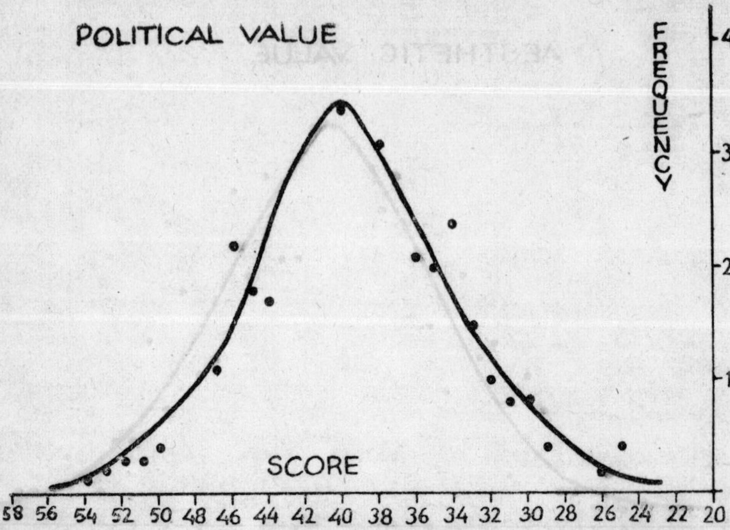

Appendix A Chart 12

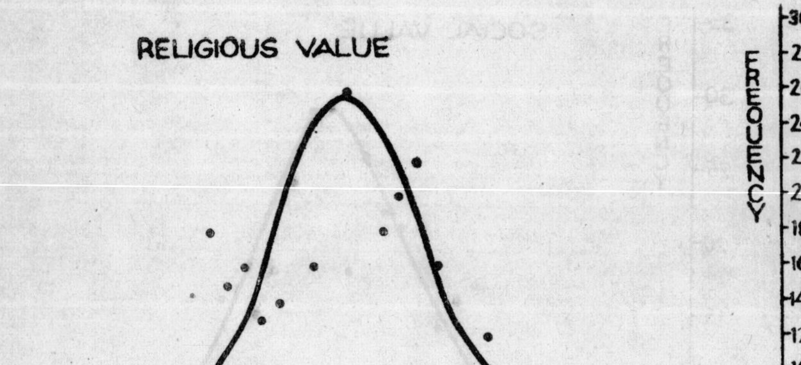

Appendix A Chart 13

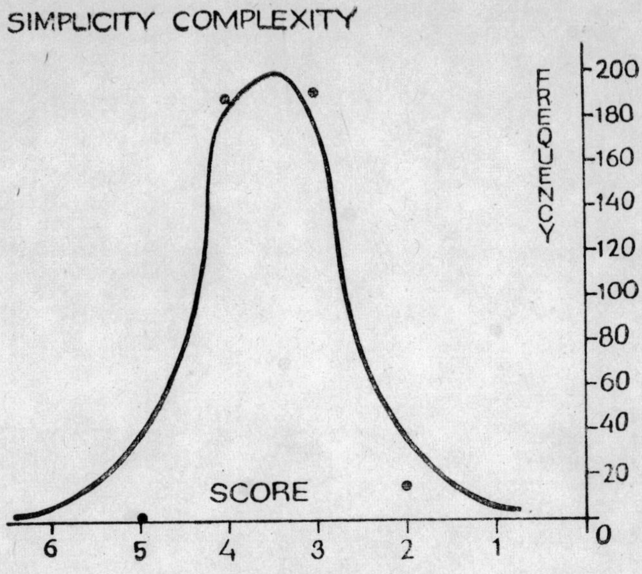

Appendix A Chart 14

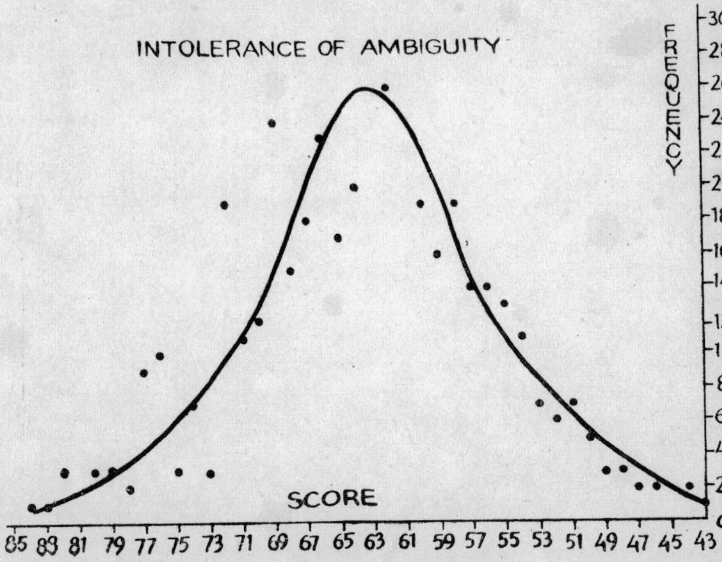

Appendix A Chart 15

Bibliography

Akinboye, Julius O. "Patterns of creativity in building engineers." *The Journal of Creative Behaviour*, 15-1-1981.

Allport, G.W. Vernon, P.E. and Lindzey, G. *Study of values : Manual of directions.* (Rev. ed.) Boston : Houghton Mifflin. 1951.

Allport, G.W., Vernon, P.E. and Lindzey, G. *Study of values : Manual.* Boston : Houghton Mifflin. 1960.

Allport, G.W., Vernon, P.E. and Lindzey, G. *Study of values : Test booklet* (Third Ed.) Boston : Houghton Mifflin. 1960a.

Allport, G.W., Vernon, P.E. and Lindzey, G. *Manual for the Study of values : A scale for measuring the dominant interests in personality.* Boston : Houghton Mifflin. 1970.

Anastasi, A. & Shaefer, C.E. "Note on the concepts of creativity and intelligence." *Journal of Creative Behaviour*, 1971, *5*, 113-116.

Bajard, G. "Validation differentielle et analyse factorielle d'une batterie de tests." *Bull. de l' I.N.O.P.* 1955, *11*, 38-58.

Barron, F. and Welsh, G.S. "Artistic perception as a possible factory in personality style : Its measurement by a figure preference test." *Journal of Psychology*, 1952, *33*, 199-203.

Barron, F. "Complexity-Simplicity as a personality dimension." *J. Abnorm. Soc. Psychol.*, 1953a, *68*, 163-172.

Barron, F. "Some personality correlates of independent judgment." *J. Personality,* 1953b, *48*, 287-297.

Barron, Frank "Some relationships between originality and style of personality." *American Psychologist*, 1954, *IX*, pp. 326.

Barron, Frank "The disposition towards originality." *Journal of Abnormal and Social Psychology*, 1955, *LI*, pp. 478-485.

Barron, F. "The psychology of imagination." *Scientific American*, 1958, 199 : *3* : 150-170.

Barron, F. *Creativity and Psychological Health : Origins of personality and creative freedom*, Princeton, N.J. : Van Nostrand, 1963(a).

Barron, F. "The needs for order and disorder as motives in creative activity." In Taylor, C.W. and Barron, F. (eds.), *Scientific Creativity.* New York : Wiley, 1963(b).

Barron, F. "The psychology of creativity." In *New Directions in Psychology* II. New York : Holt, Rinehart and Winston, 1965.

Barron, F. *Creative person and creative process.* New York : Holt, Rinehart and Winston, Inc. 1969.

Barron, F. "The inheritance of aesthetic judgment and creative thinking abilities." *Acta Geneticae Medicae et Gemellologiae.* 1970, 19(1).

Barron, Frank "An eye more fantastical." In Davis, Gary A. and Scott, Joseph A. (eds.). *Training Creative Thinking.* Holt, Rinehart and Winston, Inc. 1971.

Barron, F. Travels in search of new latitudes for innovation. In Taylor, Calvin W. (ed.). *Climate for Creativity.* Pergamon Press, 1972.

Belbin, R.M. *Management Teams : Why they Succeed or Fail,* London : Heinemann, in press, 1981.

Bennett, G.K. "Manual, Mechanical Comprehension Test, Form AA." New York : The Psychological Corporation, 1947.

Bensburg, G.J. and Sloan, W. "The use of the Cattell Culture Free Test with mental defectives." *Amer. J. Ment. Defec.*, 1955, *59*, 499-503.

Bennett, George R. *Bennett Test of Mechanical Comprehension* (New York : Psy. Corp., 1956).

Blade, M.F. "Creativity in engineering." In Coler, M.A. (Ed.). *Essays on creativity in the sciences.* New York : New York University Press, 1963.

Blatt, S.J. and Stein, M.T. Some personality, value, and cognitive characteristics of the creative person. *Amer. J. Psychol.*, 1957, *12*, 406.

Bloom, B S. "Report on creativity research by the examiner's office of the University of Chicago." In Taylor, C.W. & Barron, F. (eds.). *Scientific Creativity : Its recognition and development.* New York : Wiley, 1963.

Box, G.E.P. "Non-normality and tests on variances. Biometrika, 1953, 40, 318-335.

Buch, M.B. *A survey of research in education.* Baroda : 1974.

Budner, S. Intolerance of ambiguity as a personality variable. *Journal of Personality*, 1962, *30*, 29-50.

Buel, W.D. and Bachner, V.M. The assessment of creativity in a research setting. *J. Appl. Psychol.*, 1961, *45*, 353-358.

Buel, W.D. Biographical data and the identification of creative research personnel. *J. Appl Psychol.*, 1965, *49*, 318-321.

Buhl, Harold R. "Engineering creativity ; qualities of the creative engineering student," Department of Mechanical Engineering, Iowa State College, September, 1958.

Buros, O.K. *The Fifth Mental Measurements Year Book.* New Jersey : The Gryphon Press, 1959.

Buros, Oscar Krisen (ed.). *The Sixth Mental Measurements Year Book.* 1965, pp 1136-1137.

Burt, C. "Critical notice of 'Creativity and Intelligence' by Getzels and Jackson." *British Journal of Educational Psychology*, 1962, *32*, 292-298.

Callistor, J. "Individual differences in cognitive style : Preference for complexity-simplicity." M. Sc. thesis, University of Aston. 1970.

Cattell, R.B. and Cattell, A.K.S. "Culture Fair Intelligence Test." Scale 3 Illinois : Institute for Personality and Ability Testing, 1959.

Cattell, R.B., Feingold, S.N. and Sarason, S.B. A culture free intelligence test. II. Evaluation of cultural influences on test performance. *J. Educ. Psychol.*, 1941, 32, 81-100.

Cattell, R.B., Eber, H.W. & Tatsuoka, M.M. *Handbook for the Sixteen Personality Factor Questionnaire*, Champaign : IPAT, 1970.

Chambers, Jack A. "Beginning a multidimensional theory of creativity." *Psychological Reports,* 1969, *25*, 779-799.

Chambers, J.A. College teachers : Their effect on the creativity of students (Final Report, Project No. 9-D-046, Grant No. OEG-Y-9-190046-0057-057, NCERD, HEW.) Tampa, Elorida : University of South Florida, March, 1972.

Chawla, Tilak R. "Construction of a Perceptual Simplicity-Complexity Test." *Journal of Psychological Researches,* 1970, 14, 1.

Chorness, M.H. and Nottlemann, D.A. "The predictability of creative expression in teaching," Air Force Personnel and Training Research Centre, Lackland Air Force Base, December, 1956.

Cicirelli, V.G. "The relationship between measures of creativity, IQ, and academic achievement : interaction and threshold effects." *Doctoral dissertation,* University of Michigan, 1964.

Clifford, P.I. "Emotional contacts with the external world manifested by a selected group of highly creative chemists and mathematicians." *Perceptual and Motor Skills,* 1958, *8*, 3-26 (Monogr. Suppl. V 8-2).

Convington, M.V., Crutchfield, R.S., & Davies, Lillian B. *The productive thinking programme.* Berkeley, California : Braztonel Printing Co., 1966, 633.

Crawford, R.P. *The techniques of creative thinking*. New York : Hawthorn, 1954.

Cropley, A.J. "Creativity and intelligence." *Brit. J. Educ. Psychol.*, 1966, *36*, 259-266).

Cropley, A.J. and Maslany, G.W. "Reliability and factorial validity of the Wallach-Kogan creativity tests." *Brit. J. Psychol*, 1969, 60, 395-398.

Crutchfield, Richard. "The creative process." In *Proceedings of Conference on the creative person.* Institute of Personality Assessment and Research, University of California, Berkeley,

California, 1961, pp. VI-14.

Davis, G.A., Manske, M.E., & Train, A.J. "Training creative thinking." Occasional paper no. 6, Wisconsin Research and Development Centre, University of Wisconsin, Madison, WI, 1967.

Decay, J.S. and Madaus, G.F. "An analysis of two hypotheses concerning the relationship between creativity and intelligence." *Journal of Educational Research*, 1971, *64*, 214-16.

Dellas, Marie and Gaier, Eugene, L. "Identification of creativity : The individual." *Psychological Bulletin*, 1970, 73, *1*, 55-73.

Dentler, R.A. & Mackler, B. "Originality : some social and personal determinants." *Behavioural Science*, 1964, *9*, 1-7.

DeSimone, D. V. Introduction. In DeSimone, D.V. (ed). *Education for Innovation*. London : Oxford, 1968.

Drevdahl, J.E. "Some developmental and environmental factors in creativity." In C.W. Taylor (ed.). *Widening horizons in creativity*. New York : Wiley. 1964.

Edwards, M.P. and Taylor, L.E. "Intelligence, creativity and achievement in a non-selective public junior high school." *Journal of Educational Psychology*, 1965, *56*, 96-99.

Eiduson, B.T. *Artist and non-artist : a comparative psychological study*. Doctoral dissertation, University of California. 1957.

Eiduson, B.T. "Artist and non-artist : a comparative study." *J. Personality*, 1958, *26*, 13-28.

Eiduson, B.T. *Scientists—their psychological world*. New York : Basic Books, 1962.

Eisenman, R. & Robinson, N. "Complexity-simplicity, creativity, intelligence and other correlates." *Journal of Psychology*, 1967, *67*, 331-334.

Eisenman, R. and Schussel, N.R. "Creativity, birth order and preference for symmetry." *Journal of Consulting and Clinical Psychology*, 1970, *34* : 275-280.

Elliott, A.G.P. Fakers. "A Study of Managers' responses on a personality test." *Personnel Review*, 5, *1*, 1976.

Fee, F. "An alternative to Ward's factor analysis of Wallach and Kogan's 'creativity' correlations." *Brit. J. Educ. Psychol*, 1968, *38*, 319-321.

Fleming, E.S. and Weintraub, S. "Additional rigidity as a measure of creativity in gifted children." *Journal of Educational Psychology*, 1962, *53*, 81-85.

Flescher, I. "Anxiety and achievement of intellectually gifted and creatively gifted children." *Journal of Psychology*, 1963, *56*, 251-268.

Frantx, N.R., Jr. "An investigation of the relationship between creative thinking and mechanical reasoning among eighth grade students." Unpublished master's thesis, University of Maryland, 1964.

Frankel-Brunswik, Else. "Intolerance of ambiguity as an emotional and perceptual personality variable." *J. Pers.*, 1949, *18*, 108-143.

Frankel-Brunswik, Else. "Personality theory and perception." In, Blake, R.R., and Ramsey, G.V. (ed.). *Perception : An approach to personality*. New York : Ronald Press, 1951.

Fromm, Erich. "The creative attitude." In *Creativity and its cultivation*, (ed.), Harold H. Anderson (New York : Harper and Row, 1959), 44-54.

Gakhar, S. and Kaura, Neelam. "Creativity-intelligence : A study of structural relationship and threshold hypothesis." *Creativity Newsletter* 6, 1, February 1977, 27-37.

Geist, H. "Evaluation of culture free intelligence." *Calif. J. Educ. Res.*, 1954, *5*, 209-214.

Getzels, J.W. and Csikszentmihalyi, M. "Creative thinking in art students – an exploratory study." University of Chicago, report CRP-E-008, 1964.

Getzels, J.W. & Csikszentmihalyi, M. "Creativity in Art Students : Personality, Cognition and the Process of Discovery." Paper presented at the annual meeting of the American Psychological Association, Chicago, September, 1965.

Getzels, J.W. & Jackson, P.W. "The meaning of 'giftedness'— an examination of an expanding concept." *Phi Delta Kappan*, 1958, *40*, 75-77.

Getzels, J.W. & Jackson, P.W. "Family environment and cognitive style : a study of sources of highly intelligent and highly creative adolescents." *American Sociological Review*, 1961, *26*, 351-359.

Getzels, J.W. & Jackson, P.W. *Creativity and intelligence*, New York : Wiley, 1962.

Ginsberg, G.P., & Whittemore, R.G. "Creativity and verbal ability : A direct examination of their relationship." *British Journal of Educational Psychology*, 1968, *38*, 133-139.

Golann, S.E. "The creativity motive" *Journal of Personality*, 1962, *30*, 588-600.

Golann, S.E. "Psychological study of creativity." *Psychological Bulletin*, 1963, *60*, 548-565.

Goodyear. Seminar on the "Promotion of the creative activities of engineers", Prague, Sept. 1979.

Gopal, Arun Kumar. "Certain differentiating personality variables of creative and non-creative science and engineering students." Unpublished Ph. D. Thesis, Kurukshetra University, 1974.

Gordon, W.J.J. Synectics. New York : Horper & Row, 1961.

Gough, H.G. "The adjective checklist as a personality assessment research technique." *Psychological Reports. Monograph Suppliment*, 1960, *6*, 107-122.

Gough, H.G. "Techniques of identifying the creative research scientist." In Mackinnon, D.W. (ed.)., *The creative person.* Berkeleys : University of California Exten., 1961.

Gowan, J.C. "Development process and its guidance implications." *California Personnel and Guidance Association Journal*, *1* : 18-22, Winter 1968-69.

Goyal, R.P. "A study of some personality traits of high creative children at school stage. *Indian Educational Review*. 1972, 7, *2*, 92-100.

Graves, M.E. The *art of color and design*. New York : McGraw Hill, 1951.

Gregory, S.A. "Creativity and innovation." *The Chemical Engineer*, 1971, *250*, 229-240.

Gregory S.A. *Creativity and innovation in engineering*. London ; Butterworths. 1972.

Gregory, S.A. "Engineering, creativity and innovation : definition and measurement." In Gregory, S.A. *Creativity and innovation in engineering.* London : Butterworths, 1972.

Guilford, J.P. "Creativity." *Amer. Psychologist*, 1950, *5* : 444-454.

Guilford, J.P. *Psychological methods.* New York : McGraw Hill, 1954.

Guilford, J.P. "The nature of creativity." *Res. Bull.*, Eastern Arts Assn., 1954.

Guilford, J.P. "The structure of intellect." *Psychological Bulletin*, 1956, *53*, 267-293.

Guilford, J.P. "The dimension of aptitude." *Personality.* New York : McGraw Hill, 1959.

Guilford, J.P. "Three faces of intellect." *Amer. Psychologist*, 1959a, *14* : 469-479.

Guilford, J.P. "Potentiality for creativity and its measurement." *In Proceedings of the 1962 invitational conference on testing problem.* Princeton : Educational testing service, 1962a.

Guilford, J.P. "Parameters and categories of talent." In *The Year Book of Education.* London : Evans Brothers, 1962b.

Guilford, J.P. "Intelligence : 1965 model." *Amer. Psychologist*, 1966b, *21* : 20-26.

Guilford, J.P. "The nature of human intelligence," New York : McGraw-Hill, 1967.

Guilford, J.P. "Executive functions and a model of behaviour." *Journal of General Psychology*, 1972, *86* : 279-287.

Guilford, J.P., and Christensen, P.R. "A factor analytic study of verbal fluency." *Rep. Psychol. Lab.* 17, Los Angeles : Univer. Southern California, 1956.

Guilford, J.P., Christensen, P.R., Frick, J.W. and Merrifield, P.R. "A factor analytic study of flexibility in thinking, 1957."

Guilford, J.P., & Merrified, P.R. "The structure of intellect model : its uses and applications." *Rep. Psychol. Lab.*, Los Angeles : University of Southern Calif., 1960, 24.

Gust, T. "The creativity dimension in counselor effectiveness." Doctoral dissertation, North Dakota State Univer. Cited in Torrance, E.P. (1967) The Minnesota studies of creative behaviour ; National and international extensions. *J. Creative*

Behaviour, 1964, *1*, 137-154.

Hacker, F.J. "Creative possibilities for a consideration of creativity." In Anderson, H.H. (ed.). *Creativity in childhood and adolescence.* California : Science and Behaviour Books, Inc., 1965.

Hachn, M. *Review of research on creativity.* Minneapolis : University of Minnesota Press, 1968.

Hallman, R.J. "The necessary and sufficient conditions of creativity," *Journal of Humanistic Psychology*, 3 : *1*, Spring 1963 (Also reprinted in J.C. Gowan and others, *Creativity : its Educational Implications*, New York : John Wiley & Co., 1967).

Hall, W.B. and Mackinnon, D.W. "Personality inventory correlates of creativity among architects." *Journal of Applied Psychology*, 1969, *53*, 4,322-326.

Harris, Richard H. "The development and validation of a test of creative ability," Doctoral Dissertation Series, Publication No. 13, 927, University Microfilms, Ann Arbor, Michigan, 1955.

Hart, H.H. "The integrative function in creativity," *Psychiatric Quarterly*, 1950, 24, *1*, 1-16.

Hartston, W.R. *The Personal Preference Questionnaire; a User's Manual*, Cambridge : ITRU (undated).

Hasan, P. and Butcher, H.J. "Creativity and intelligence. A partial replication with Scottish children of Getzel's and Jackson's study." *British Journal of Psychology*, 1966, *57*, 129-135.

Hasan, Qumar *Dogmatism and personality.* Calcutta : Temple Press, 1974.

Heist, P. "Considerations in the assessment of creativity." In Heist P. (ed.). *The creative college student : An unmet challenge.* San Francisco : Jossey - Bass, 1968.

Helson, R. & Crutchfield, R.S. "Mathematicians, the creative researcher and the average Ph.D." *Journal of Consulting & Clinical Psychology*, 1970, *34*, 250-257 (b).

Henninger, G. Ross and Houghton, E. "Comments concerning technical education in India." In *Report of the Special*

Committee on Re-organisation and Development of Polytechnic Education in India. 1970-71 72-77.

Herr, E.L., Moore, G.D. and Hansen, J.C. "Creativity, intelligence and values : A study of relationships mimeo.)" State University of New York at Buffalo, 1965.

Hudson, L. *Contrary Imagination,* London : Methuen, 1966.

Irvine, F.R. "A study of creative thinking ability and its relationship to psychomotor ability, mechanical reasoning ability and vocational attitude of selected high school industrial arts students." (Doctoral Dissertation, Utah State University, 1968) Dissertation Abstracts International, 1968, *29A* : 1768. (University Microfilms Order No. 68-13, 748.

Jha, S.K. "An analysis of certain dimensions of creativity." Bombay : Himalaya Publishing House, 1978.

Kaiser, Aluminium News (you and creativity), 1968, *25*, 3-39.

Khatena, J. "Some problems in the measurement of creative behaviour." *Journal of Research and Development in Education,* 1971, *4*, 74-82.

Krick, E.V. *An introduction to engineering and engineering design,* John Wiley, 1965.

Kubie, L.S. *Neurotic distortion of the creative process.* Lawrence ; Kansas Press, 1958.

Kuhn, T.S. "The essential tension : Tradition and innovation in scientific research." In Taylor, C.W. & Barron, F (eds.). *Scientific creativity* : Its recognition and development. New York : Wiley, 1963.

Kumar, Girijesh "Creative functioning in relation to personality, value-orientation and achievement motivation." *Indian Educational Review.* 1978, XIII, 2, 110-115.

Kundu, C. *Personality development a critique of Indian studies.* Vishal, 1977.

Lawshe, C.H. & Harris, D.H. "Purdue Creativity Test—Manual of instructions." West Lafayette, Indiana : Purdue Research Foundation, 1960.

Levinson, D.J. and Sanford, R.N. "A scale for the measurement of anti-semitism." *J. Psychol.*, 1944, *17*, 339-370.

Lindgren, H.C., & Lindgren, F. "Brainstorming and orneriness as facilitators of creativity." *Psychological Reports*, 1965, *16*, 577-583.

Lindquist, E.F. *Statistical analysis in education*. Boston : 1940.

Lovell, K. and Shields, J.B. "Some aspects of a study of the gifted child." *British Journal of Educational Psychology*, 1967, 37.

MacCurdy, Robert D. "Scientist or Engineer ?" *Journal of Counselling Psychology*, *8* : 79-81, Spring, 1961.

MacKinnon, D.W. "Creativity in architects." In MacKinnon, D.W. (ed.). *The creative person, Berkeley* : Institute of Personality Assessment Research, Univer. of California, 1961, V-1-V-24 (B).

MacKinnon, D.W., *et al. Proceedings of the conference on "The creative person"*, Univer. of California Alumni Center, Lake Tahoe, California. Berkeley : University of California Extension, 1961.

MacKinnon, D.W. "The study of creativity and creativity in architects." In *Conference on the creative person*. Berkeley : University of California, 1961.

MacKinnon, D.W. "The nature and nurture of creative talent." *American Psychologist*, 1962—a, *17*, 484-495.

MacKinnon, D.W. "The personality correlates of creativity : A study of American architects." In Nielsen, G.S. (ed.). Proceedings of the XIV International Congress of Applied Psychology, Copenhagen, 1961. Copenhagen : Munksgaard, 1962, 2, 11-39 (b).

MacKinnon, D.W. "Identifying and developing creativity." *Journal of Secondary Education*, 1963, *38*, 166-174.

MacKinnon, D.W. "Education for creativity : A modern myth ?" In P. Heist (ed.). *Education for creativity in the American college*. University of California : Center for Research and Development in Higher Education, 1967.

MacKinnon, D.W. "The courage to be : Realising Creative potential," 1969 (Mimeographed).

Maddi, S.R. "Motivational aspects of creativity." *Journal of personality*, 1965, *33*, 330-347.

Mallappa, K.R. & Upadhyaya, Ramesh. "Creativity and Personality." *Indian Psychological Review*. 1977, *14*, *2*, 31-35.

Maltzman, I. "On the training of originality." *Psychological Review*, 1960, *67*, 229-242.

Marquant, D. I. and Bailey, L.L. "An evaluation of the culture free test of intelligence." *J. Genet Psychol.*, 1955, *86*, 353-358.

Marsh, R.W. "A statistical re-analysis of Getzels and Jackson's data." *British Journal of Educational Psychology*, 1964, *34*, 91-93.

Maslow, A.H. "Emotional blocks to creativity." *Journal of Individual Psychology*, 1958, *14* : 51-56.

Maslow, A.H. *Toward a psychology of being*. Princeton : D. Van Nostrand, 1962.

Maslow, A.H. "A holistic approach to creativity." In Taylor, Calvin W. (ed.). *Climate for creativity*. New York : Pergamon Press, 1972.

Mason, J.G. *How to be a more creative cxecutive*. NYC : McGraw-Hill, 1960.

McClelland, D.C. "On the psychodynamics of creative physical scientists." In Gruber, H.E., Terrell, G. and Wertheimer, M. (eds.). *Contemporary approaches to creative thinking*. New York : Atherton Press, 1962, 141-74.

McDermid, Charles D. "Some correlates of creativity in engineering personnel." *Journal of Applied Psychology*, 49 (1964) 14-19.

McNemar, Q. "Lost : Our intelligence why" ? *American Psychologist*, 1964, *19*, 871-882.

McPherson, J.H. "A proposal for establishing ultimate criteria for measuring creative output." In *Scientific Creativity : its recognition and development*, New York : Wiley 1963.

Mcpherson, J.H. *The People, the Problems and the Problem Solving Methods*, Midland : Michigan, Pendell, 1967.

Mednick, S.A. "The associative basis of the creative process." *Psychological Review*, 1962, *69*, 220-232.

Mednick, M.T. & Andrews, F.M. "Creative thinking and level of intelligence." *The Journal of Creative Behavior*, 1967, *1*, 428-431.

Meer, B. and Stein, M.I. "Measures of intelligence and creativity." *Journal of Psychology*, 1955, *39*, 117-126.

Mehdi, Baqer. "Creativity, intelligence and achievement : some findings of recent research." *Indian Educational Review*, 1974, *9*, *1*, 1-9.

Merrifield, Phillip R. "Purdue Creativity Test—Applicants for engineering positions." In Buros, O.K. (ed.). *The Sixth Mental Measurements* Year Book, 1965.

Merrifield, P. "How an educational psychologist views the creative process." *Educator*, 1976, *18*, *2*, 16TEEN-22WO.

Misra, H.K. "Personality factors in high and low achievers in engineering education, Ph. D." Education, Indian Institute of Technology, Kharagpur, 1962.

Mitra, S.K. "A survey of research in psychology, (ICSSR)" Bombay : Popular Prakashan, 1972.

Mitra S.K. Foreword. Needs and priorities in creativity research New Delhi : National Institute of Education, 1975.

Moffie, D.J. "A predictive validity study of creative and effective managerial performance". The Creativity Research Institute of Smith Richardson Foundation, Inc. November, 1968.

Mooney R.L. "A conceptual model for integrating four approaches to the identification of creative talent." Research Conference on the Identification of Creative - Scientific Talent, University of Utah, 1957.

Mooney, Boss L. and Razik, Taher, A. *Explorations in creativity*. New York : Harper & Row, 1967.

Myden, W. "Interpretation and evaluation of certain personality characteristics involved in creative production." *Percept. Motor Skills*, 1959, *9*, 139-158

Myers, R.E., & Torrance, E.P. *Invitations to thinking and doing*. Boston : Ginn, 1965.

Myers, R.E., & Torrance, E.P. *Invitations to speaking and writing creatively*. Boston : Ginn, 1965(a).

Myers, R.E., & Torrance, E.P. *Can you imagine* ? Boston : Ginn, 1965(b).

Myers, R.E., & Torrance, E.P. *Plots, puzzles, and plays.* Boston : Ginn, 1966(a).

Myers, R.E., & Torrance, E.P. *For these who wonder.* Boston : Ginn, 1966(b).

Nagarajan, R. "Creative engineering design-How to induce creativity." *Proceedings of Seminar on Creative Engineering Design.* IIT, Madras, 1973, 37-44.

National Conference on Creative Engineering Education, 1965.

Nicholls, John G. "Creativity : Sense and nonsense." *Educator.* 1976, 18, *2*, 23HREE - 28IGHT.

Nie, Norman H. *et. al. Statistical package for the Social Sciences* (SPSS). New York : Mc Graw-Hill, 1975.

Offner, D.H. "Energizing the creative potential in future engineers." *The Journal of Creative Behaviour,* 1967, 1, 15-21.

Osborn, A.F. "Applied Imagination" (3rd ed.). New York : Scribner, 1963.

Owens, W.A. "Cognitive, noncognitive and environmental correlates of mechanical ingenuity," *Journal of Applied Psychology,* 1969, 53, *3*, 199-208.

Owens, W.A. "Intellective, non-intellective and environmental correlates of mechanical ingenuity." In Taylor, Calvin W. (ed.). *Climate for Creativity.* New York : Pergamon Press, 1972.

Owens, W.A. ; Schumacher, C.F. and Clark, J.B. "The measurement of creativity in Machine Design," *Report of Research Conference on the Identification of Creative Scientific Talent,* University of Utah, August 17-20, 1957, 129-140.

Pal, S.K. "Values of students in four professions under Indian conditions." *Journal of Social Psychology,* 1967 a, *72,* 297-298.

Pal, S.K. "Personality needs of engineering, law, medical and teacher-training students in an Indian university." *Journal of Social Psychology,* 1968, a, *74,* 135.

Pal S.K. "Personality patterns of engineering, law, medical and teacher - training students : A comparative study", *Journal of Social Psychology* 1968b, *74,* 287-288.

Pal, S.K. "Personality adjustment of engineering and medical students," *Indian Journal of Applied Psychology*, 1963c, 5(*1*), 82-84.

Paramesh, C.R. "Value orientations of creative persons." *Psychol. studies*, 1970, *15*, 108-113.

Paramesh, C.R. *Creativity and personality.* Madras : Janatha Publishing Co., 1972.

Parnes, S.J. *Workbook for creative problem solving institutes and courses.* Buffalo : Creative Education Foundation, 1966.

Pepinsky, Pauline N. "A study of productive non-conformity," *Gifted Child Quarterly*, 1960, *4*, 81-85.

Perry, J.M. "Correlation of teacher prediction for student success six years beyond sixth grade." *Doctoral dissertation*, University of Illinois. 1966.

Pestonjee, D.M. and Akhtar, S.S. "Occupational values, preferences and income aspirations of engineering and teacher training students," *Indian Psychological Review*, 1969, 5(*2*), 131-135.

Radhakrishnan, S. *Occasional speeches and writings.* Delhi: The Publication Division, 1960.

Raina, M.K. "Applied Creativity : The creative studies project at the University of Buffalo," Creativity Newsletter, Aligarh, 2, *2*, 1973, 1-4.

Raina M.K. "Creativity Research in India : An analysis." *The Journal of Creative Behavior*, 1969, *3*, 200-210.

Raina, M.K. and Shukla, J.K. "Personality and motivational measures of creativity." *Creativity and Undergraduate Science Education*. 1972, 90-113.

Raina M.K. *Creativity : An annotated bibliography*. Unpublished.

Raina, M.K. "Creativity in India : A survey." *UCLA Educator* Spring 1976, 18, *2*, 59INE-67EVEN.

Rawat, M.S. and Agarwal, Saroj "A study on creative thinking." *Indian Psychological Review* 14, *2*, 1977, 36-40.

Raychaudhuri, M. "Complexity-Simplicity dimension and perceptual preference pattern of the musician and non-musician." Proc. 49th session, Ind. Sc. Cong. Assoc. 1962, Part III, 512-513.

Raychaudhuri, M. "Some perceptual characteristic of incipient artists." *Ind. J. Psychol.*, 1963, 38, 13-17.

Raychoudhuri, M. "Personality correlates of creativity" *Samiksha*, 1965(b).

Raychaudhari, "Manas Aesthetic interest, education, Millieu difference, and tolerance of ambiguity." *Archivos Panamenos De Psicologia*, Panama City 1966.

Raychaudhuri, M. "Creativity and personality : A review of psychological researches." *Indian Psychological Review*, 1966, *2*, 91-102(a).

Raychaudhuri, M. "Perceptual preference pattern and creativity." *Indian Journal of Applied Psychology*, 1966, *3*, 67-70(b)

Reid, J.B., King, F.J. and Wickwire, P. "Cognitive and other personality characteristics of creative children." *Psychol. Rep.*, 1959, *5*, pp. 729-738.

Repucci, L.C. "What research reveals about creativity." In Davis A Gary and Scott A. Joseph. Training creative thinking. New York : Holt, Rinehart and Winston, Inc., 1971.

Richards, J.M., Cline, V.B. and Needham, W.F. "Creativity tests and achievement in high school science." *Journal of Applied Psychology*, 1963, *47*, 184-9.

Ripple, R.E. and May, F.B. "Caution in comparing creativity and IQ." *Psychol. Rep.* 1962, *10*, 229-230.

Rodd, W.G. "A cross-cultural study of Taiwan's schools." Ph. D. Thesis, Western Reserve University Library, 1958.

Roe, A. "Psychological study of physical scientists. *Genetic Psychology Monographs*, 1951, *43* (2) : 121-235.

Roe, A. *The making of a scientist*. New York : Dodd, Mead. 1953.

Roe, A. *The Psychology of occupations*. New York : Wiley. 1956.

Rogers, C.R. "Toward a theory of creativity. In Parnes, S.J. & Harding, H.F. (eds.). *A source book for creative thinking*, NYC : Scribner, 1962, 63-72.

Rosen, J.C. "The Barron-Welsh Art Scale as a predictor of originality and level of ability among artists." *Journal of Applied Psychology*, 1955, *39*, 366-367.

Rosen, C.G.A. "In quest of engineering creativeness. *Jcurral of Engineering Education*, 1958, *48*, 917-922.

Rosten, Leo. "The creative idea." *Teachers College Record*, 1963, 637-646.

Roweton, W.E. "Creativity : A Review of theory and research." *The creative education foundation.* Occasional Paper Number 7, 1973, 1-25.

Saran, Y. "Preface : country course on institution building processes—a monograph." Technical Teachers Training Institute, Bhopal, 1977.

Schaefer, C.E. "The self-concept of creative adolescents." *Journal of Psychology*, 1969, *72*(*2*), 233-242.

Schroeder, H.M., Driver, M.J., & Streufert, S. *Himan Information Processing.* New York : Holt, Rinehart, & Winston, 1967.

Secretary of State for Industry : *Engineering Our Future*, Report of the Committee of Inquiry into the Engineering Profession. Chairman, Sir Montague Finniston FRS. Comnd. 7794, London : HMSO, 1980, 258.

Sen Gupta, M. "Personality characteristics of creative engineers : A review of researches." *Journal of Indian Education*, 1976, *3*, 26-33.

Sen Gupta, M. "Role of creativity in engineering education." *Indian Psychological Review*, 1977, *14*, 48-50.

Shanker, Uma. "An experimental study of reactive inhibition and some personality variable." A Ph. D. dissertation. Patna University, 1970.

Singh, Ram Janam. "Training for Creatity—A Critical Review," *Journal of Education and Psychology*, XXXIII, *4*, 1976.

Sinha, D. and Misra, H.K. "Qualities desirable for engineering students and profession (Part I : teachers' sample)." *Journal of Psychological Researches*, 1961a, *5*(*1*), 1-12.

Sinha, D. and Misra, H.K. "Qualities desirable for engineering students and profession," (Part II : students' sample), *Journal of Psychological Researches.* 1961b, *6*.

Sinha, D. and Misra, H.K. "Qualities desirable for engineering students and profession," (Part III : Comparison of teachers' and students' sample), *Journal of Psychological Researches*, 1963, *7*, 16-20.

Smith, R.M. "Characteristics of creativity research," *Perceptual and Motor Skills*. 1968, *26*, 698.

Snyder, B. "Creative students in science and engineering." *Universities Quarterly*, 1967, *21*, *2*, 204-218.

Spearman, C. *The Creative mind*. New York : Appleton-Century Crofts, 1931.

Staats, A.W. "Learning, language, and cognition." NYC : Holt, Rinehart, and Winston, 1968.

Stein, M.I. "Creativity and culture." *Journal of Psychology*, 1953, *36*, 311-322.

Stein, Morris I., and Meer, Bernard. "Perceptual organization in a study of creativity," *Journal of Psychology*, 1954, 39-43.

Steinberg, Leonard "Creativity as a character trait : An expanding concept," In Gowan, J.C. *et al. Creativity : Its educational implications*. Ne York : John Wiley & Sons, Inc. 1967.

Steiner, Gary A. *The Creative Organization*. Selected Paper No. 2, Proceedings of Seminar, Graduate school of business, Chicago : University of Chicago Press, 1962.

Swani, N.M. Welcome address, *Proceedings of the golden jubilee session of association of Indian universities*, 1975, XI-XIII.

Taylor, C.W. *The Identification of creative scientific talent*. Salt Lake City, Utah : Univer. of Utah Press. 1955.

Taylor, Donald W. "Variables related to creativity and productivity among men in two research laboratories," Report prepared under Project NR 150-149 and supported by Contract N60 nr 25125 between Stanford University and the Office of Naval Research, 1958.

Taylor, C.W. (e.d). *Creativity Progress and potential*. New York : McGraw-Hill, 1964.

Terman, L.M. "Intelligence and its measurement : A symposium" *Jr. Educ. Psychol*. 1921, *12*, 127-133.

Terman, L.M. "Scientists and nonscientists in a group of 800 gifted men." *Psychological Monographs* : General and Applied. 1954, 68(7) : 1-44 (Whole No. 378).

Terman. L.M. "Are scientists different"? *Scientific American.* 1955, 192(1) : 25-29.

Thomson, S.G. *The factorial analysis of human ability.* London : Univer. of London Press Ltd. 1951.

Thomson, S.G. *The factorial analysis of human ability.* Univer. of London Press, 1956.

Thorndike, R.L. "Some methodological issues in the study of creativity." In *proceedings of the 1962 international conference on testing problems.* Princeton, N.J. Educational Testing Service, 1963.

Thorndike, R.L. "Some methodological issues in the study of creativity." In Anastasi, (ed.). *Testing problems in perspective.* Washington, D.C. : American Council on Edu., 1966.

Thring, M.W. "The encouragement and development of originality and inventiveness in engineering students." *International Journal of Educational Sciences*, 1968, *2*, 195-199.

Thurstone, L.L. "Creative talent, Report from the Scientific Laboratory" No. 61, Chicago : University of Chicago, 1950.

Tilton, J.R. "A survey of the reliability, validity and usefulness of the Cattell Culture Free Test," *Persona.*, 1949, *1*, 17-19.

Tondon, B.K. "A study of attitude towards religion of higher secondary students in U.P. towns," Unpublished Ph. D. Thesis Education, Agra Univer., 1967.

Torrance, E.P. "Explorations in creative thinking in the early school years." VI Highly intelligent and highly creative children in laboratory school. Minneapolis : Bur. Educ. Res., Univer. Minnesota, 1959a.

Torrance, E.P. "Explorations in creative thinking in the early school years." VIII I.Q. and creativity in school achievement. Minneapolis : Bur. Educ. Res., Univer. Minnesota, 1959b.

Torrance, E.P. "Educational achievement of the highly intelligent and the highly creative : eight practical replications of the Getzels-Jackson study." Minneapolis : Bur. Educ. Research, Univer. Minnesota, 1960.

Torrance, E.P. "Guiding creative talent." Englewood Cliffs, N.J. : Prentice-Hall, 1962.

Torrance, E.P. "Measurement and development of creative thinking abilities." In *The Yearbook of Education*. London : Evans Brothers, 1962a.

Torrance, E.P. "The creative personality and the ideal pupil." *Teachers College Record*, 1963, *65*, 220-226.

Torrance, E.P. *Rewarding Creative Behavior*. Englewood Cliffs, N.J. : Prentice-Hall, 1964.

Torrance, E.P. "Scientific views of creativity and factor affecting its growth." Reprinted by permission of Daedalus, *Journal of the American Academy of Arts & Sciences*, Boston, Massachusetts, 1965, Creativity and Learning. 662-681.

Torrance, E.P. "The Minnesota studies of creative behaviour : National and international extensions." *The Journal of Creative Behaviour*, 1967, *1*(2), 137-154.

Walberg, H.J. and Welch, W.W. "Personality characteristics of innovative Physics teachers." J. *Creative Behaviour* 1967, 1, 169-171.

Walker, Eric A. "Engineers and/or Scientists : Philosophy." In Estrin, Herman, A. (ed.). *Higher Education in engineering and science*, 1963.

Walker, Helen M. and Lev, Joseph *Statistical Inference*. Calcutta : Oxford & IBH Publishing Co. 1953.

Wallach, M.A. and Kogan, N. *Modes of thinking in young children*. New York : Holt, Rinehart and Winston, 1965.

Wallach, M.A. and Kogan, N. "Creativity and intelligence in children." In J. McV. Hunt, (ed.). *Human intelligence*. 1972.

Wallach, M.A. and Kogan, N. "Creativity and intelligence in children." In Rothenberg, A. and Hausman, C.R. (ed.). *The creativity question*. Duke University Press, Durham, N.C., 1976.

Wallach, M.A. and Wing, C.W. (Jr.) *The talented student : a validation of the creativity--intelligence distinction*. New York : Holt, Rinehart & Winston, 1969.

Ward, J. "Creativity and impulsivity in kindergarten children."

Doctoral dissertation, Duke University, Durham, N.C. 1966.

Wechsler, D. *Measurment and appraisal of adult intelligence*, Williams & Wilkins, New York : 1958.

Welsh, G.S. "A projective figure-preference test for diagnosis of psychopathology : 1. A preliminary investigation." Unpublished doctoral dissertation, Univer. of Minnesota, 1949.

Welsh, G.S. "Welsh Figure Preference Test." California : Consulting Psychologists Press, 1959.

Welsh, G.S. *Creativity and intelligence : A personality approach*. Chapel hill, N.C. : Institute for Research in Social Science, 1975.

Welsh, George S. "Personality correlates of intelligence and creativity in gifted adolescents." In Stanley, J.C., George, W.C. and Solano, C.H. (ed.). *The gifted and the creative : A fifty-year perspective*. London : The John Hopkins University Press, 1977.

Whitfield, P. R. *Creativity in industry*, Harmondsworth : Penguin, 1975.

Williams, Frank E. "The search for the creative teacher." *California Teachers' Association Journal*, 60 : *1* : 14-16, 1964.

Williams, Frank E. "Creativity in engineering education," *Personnel Adminisntration*, 1966, 22-27.

Wilson, R.N. "Poetic creativity, process and personality." *Psychiatry*, 1954, 17, *2*, 163-176.

Wilson, R.C. Guilford, J.P., Christensen, R. and Lewis, D.J. "A factor analytic study of creative thinking abilities." Psychometrika, 1954, *19*, 297-311.

Windholz, G. "The relation of creativity and intelligence constellations to traits of temperament, interest and value in college students." *J. Gen. Psychol.*, 1968, *79*, 291-299.

Wodtke, K.H. "Some data on the reliability and validity of creativity tests at the elementary school level." Educ. Psychol. Measmt. 1964, *24*, 299-408.

Yamamoto, K. *Educational achievement of highly creative students : threshold of intelligence*. Research Memo, BER-

61-5. University of Minnesota, Bureau of Educational Research, 1961.

Yamamoto, K. "Relationships between creative thinking abilities of teachers and achievement and adjustment of pupils." J. Exp. Educ., 1963, *32*, 3-26.

Yamamoto, K. "Threshold of intelligence in academic achievement of highly creative students." *J. Exp. Educ.*, 1964, a, *32*, 401-405.

Yamamoto K. "Role of creative thinking and intelligence in high school achievement." *Psychol.* Rep., 1964b, *14*, 783-789.

Yamamoto, K. "A further analysis of the role of creative thinking in high school achievement," *J. Psychol.*, 1964d *58*, 277-283.

Yamamoto, K. "Effects of restriction of range and test unreliability on correlation between measures of intelligence and creative thinking." *British Journal of Educational Psychology*, 1965, *30*, 300-305.

Yamamoto, K. "Does teacher creativity make a difference in pupil learning" ? *Elementary School Journal*, 1967, 67(5), 265-270.

Zilboorg, G. "Psychology of the creative personality"." In Smith, P. (ed.). *Creativity : an examination of the creative process.* New York : Hastings House, 1959.

Index

D

E

F

R

S

T